TURNING POINTS IN HISTORY
PEOPLE
WHO CHANGED THE WORLD

Philip Wilkinson & Jacqueline Dineen
Illustrations by Robert Ingpen

CHELSEA HOUSE PUBLISHERS
New York • Philadelphia

First published in the United States by
Chelsea House Publishers, 1994

First Printing
1   3   5   7   9   8   6   4   2

Simplified text and captions by **Jacqueline Dineen**
based on the *Encyclopedia of World Events*
by Robert Ingpen & Philip Wilkinson

Editor	Diana Briscoe
Project Editor	Paul Bennett
Designer	Design 23
Design Assistant	Victoria Furbisher
DTP Manager	Keith Bambury
Editorial Director	Pippa Rubinstein

ISBN 0–7910–2764–3

Printed in Italy.

Contents

Introduction

We can all name many famous people who are alive today. The lives and faces of world leaders, from politicians to clergymen, are familiar to us from television and newspapers. But how many of these people will be well known in a few hundred years' time? Looking back it is easier to decide on at least some of the people who have had such impact that they have changed the history of the world.

Some of the most influential people have been religious leaders. Although they lived hundreds, or even thousands, of years ago, these people had a profound effect on many people during their lifetimes and in most cases their influence is still powerful. The teachings of great religious leaders, from the Chinese sage Confucius to Martin Luther, father of Protestantism, still inspire followers in different parts of the world. And the influence of religious teachings does not stop at the door of the church or temple – it reaches every part of life, from birth to our last moments.

Another group of people who have changed the world are the great explorers. Columbus and Magellan,

Buddhism is founded in India by Gautama. His disciples spread through Asia.

Jesus's teaching inspired Christianity.

Muslims, who follow Islam, conquered much land in the Near East.

530 B.C.   about A.D. 33   after 622

sailing across the world in tiny ships, or Cook taking scientists on his ships and inventing the idea of the scientific expedition, are among the best known examples. There are also the land travelers, like Marco Polo, who crossed Asia in the Middle Ages. Their journeys were great beginnings, revealing the wonders of the planet.

It seems amazing that the rulers of Athens in the fifth century B.C. should be still influencing politics today, but they were the inventors of democracy. Other turning points include the arrival of the *Mayflower* in North America, the changes in people's ideas provoked by Marx and Freud, and the U.S. Civil Rights movement. Last there are the disasters like the Black Death, the Irish Famine or the Wall Street Crash – they show humanity's amazing strength in resisting, recovering and starting again.

Philip Wilkinson

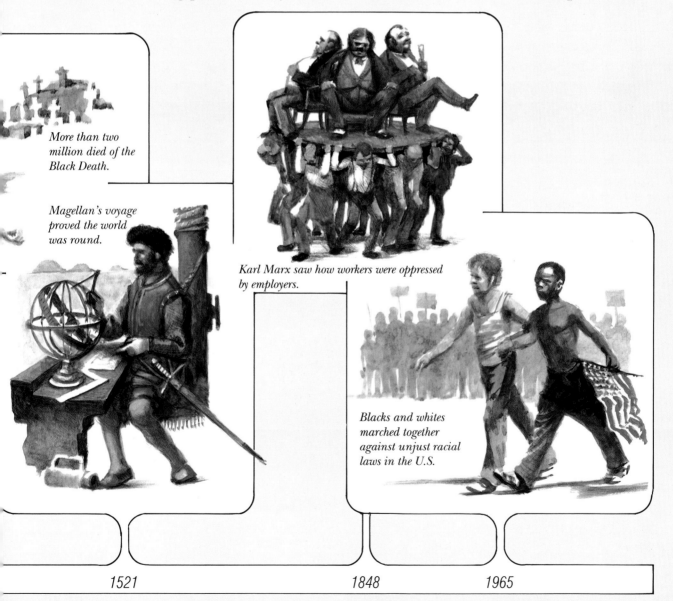

More than two million died of the Black Death.

Magellan's voyage proved the world was round.

Karl Marx saw how workers were oppressed by employers.

Blacks and whites marched together against unjust racial laws in the U.S.

1521   1848   1965

Confucius & His Thought

2,500 years ago China was a mass of warring states. Kingdom fought kingdom, and the ordinary people were oppressed and miserable. In this chaos, one man tried to formulate a code of conduct that would bring stability to his world and allow all men to live a "virtuous life." He was Confucius and his ideas still influence millions of people today.

800	400	BC/AD	400	800	1200	1600	2000

c.500 BC Lo-yang, China

Confucius was a philosopher who lived in China nearly two and a half thousand years ago. He founded one of the world's most important religions, Confucianism, and for two thousand years, he was considered to be China's greatest teacher. But who was Confucius and why did he have such an influence on Chinese thought?

Sacrifices to the spirits

We do not know very much about the Chinese civilization before about 1500 B.C. At this time, China was ruled by the Shang dynasty – a number of kings or emperors of the Shang family who ruled one after the other. The kings were related to families of nobles who reigned over the lower classes – the people who farmed the land and worked as servants.

Religion was very important to the nobles,

Confucius' (c.551–479 B.C.) thoughts and sayings became popular long after his death – Confucianism eventually became a religion and even the kings made sacrifices to him.

who worshiped Shang Ti, the main god, and the spirits of their dead ancestors. All the noble families claimed to be descended from Shang Ti, and the king was considered to be his direct descendant. The most important building in China was the temple of the royal house. It was here that the king consulted Shang Ti about everything that happened, and made sacrifices to him and to the spirits of other ancestors. Confucius was to include many features of the Shang religion in Confucianism.

Lasting impression

By the time Confucius was born in about 551 B.C., the Shang dynasty had been overthrown by the powerful Chou tribe who founded a new dynasty. The Chou dynasty made a lasting impression on Chinese history because it was a period when philosophy – the study of the meaning of the life and the way people should live – flourished.

Confucius begins to teach
Confucius' Chinese name was K'ung-Fu-tzu and his ancestors were probably nobles who had lost their riches. He was poor and life was a struggle, and so he knew what it was like to be a member of the lower classes. However, he was eager to learn, and though few books had been written, he read what he could and studied the traditions and religions of China.

Confucius began to teach what he had learned to friends and pupils. He taught that

everyone should live together in harmony, be good, honest and loyal, and have respect for their parents.

He also said that the lower classes should be ruled over with kindness rather than force. From this teaching came the Chinese tradition of the king and his officials being a "father and mother" to the people.

High rank
Confucius stressed that people should be given high rank because of their abilities, and not because they were born into a noble family. Confucius did not have a great

Above: A figure from a vast buried army of terra-cotta (clay) warriors dating to the Qin period (third century B.C.).

FASCINATING FACTS

In ancient China, soothsayers read the future with "oracle bones." These were animal bones that had cracks made in them with a heated bronze point. The soothsayers studied the cracks to work out what the gods wanted people to do and what would happen in the future.

❑

Books and documents were usually written on pieces of wood or bamboo, or sometimes on silk. Chinese writing began as pictures.

❑

About 2,000 years after their deaths, K'ung-Fu-tzu and Meng-tzu were given their Latin names, Confucius and Mencius, by Jesuit missionaries.

Some legends say that Confucius' mother had a vision telling her to go to a cave where the baby was born. Dragons and spirit maidens hovered over the cave.

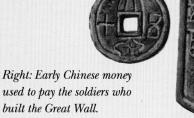

Right: Early Chinese money used to pay the soldiers who built the Great Wall.

Confucius always laid the greatest stress on family and ancestor worship. This gave rise to the respect shown for parents in traditional Chinese culture. His teaching developed into a religion, and ceremonies were established and temples were built. The emperors of China made sacrifices to Confucius and his famous disciples. The thoughts of Confucius influenced the Chinese people for over two thousand years. You can see his name in Chinese characters at the top right-hand side of this picture.

following while he was alive. He spent many years wandering about and preaching, but often people would not listen to him. However, he did not give up, saying: "Heaven has called me, and the superior man does not lose courage if the obstacles are many."

Confucius' last years

Confucius spent the last years of his life writing down his thoughts. The small group of followers who traveled with him also wrote down many of his talks and conversations. But it was not until long after his death in 479 B.C. that Confucianism became popular.

A famous teacher of Confucianism was Meng-tzu, who lived from 371 to 289 B.C. Also known as Mencius, he developed Confucius' teaching, emphasizing that goodness must win out in the end.

The work is carried on

Confucius stressed the importance of education and training, and many followers of his ideas were people who held important posts in government. When the Han dynasty took power in 202 B.C., the Confucians were the only people with the experience to manage government affairs. Through their influence, Confucianism became popular, helped by men of great learning, who spread Confucius' ideas throughout China.

Although Confucianism was concerned mainly with how people should live, it developed into a state religion and played an important part in Chinese life, particularly in training the bureaucrats who ran the empire. However, since the early twentieth century, its influence in China has declined greatly.

Gautama & Buddhism

A prince who abandoned his palace to look for enlightenment sounds like a fairy tale, but that is what Prince Siddhartha did in his search for enlightenment. The insights and spiritual truths that he found through meditation are followed by more than 500 million people today. They are the basis of one of Earth's great religions: Buddhism.

800		400	BC/AD	400	800	1200	1600	2000

c.530 BC Varanasi

At about the same time as Confucius was writing his books in China, another teacher was founding a new religion in India. Gautama, the Buddha, was seeking to teach people how to overcome suffering and understand the meaning and significance of life.

"Buddha" means "The One Who Knows." Gautama was not the first Buddha, but the way of life that he taught has influenced Asia for over 2,000 years and is found all over the world today.

Myth and legend

The Buddha's life is surrounded in myth and legend. He was born in about 563 B.C., the son of a ruler of the Shakya tribe who lived on the borders of Nepal. (Gautama was the family name.) One legend says that before he was born, his mother, Mahamaya, dreamt of a white elephant entering her womb. He was born out of her side, stood up, took seven paces and declared himself the chief of all the world.

Siddhartha Gautama (c. 563–480 B.C.). Followers of Buddhism copy his example of morality, compassion and wisdom, which led to spiritual truth – enlightenment.

The search begins

When Prince Siddhartha grew up, he married a princess called Yasodhara and they had a son, Rahula. But he became unhappy with the comfortable life he was leading and, at the age of 29, he left home and joined a group of ascetics (people who practise self-denial for religious reasons) who were searching for spiritual understanding.

He learned about meditation – deep, quiet thought – but this did not satisfy him. He and five fellow ascetics also tried going without food, thinking that the suffering would bring them enlightenment. But

Gautama became so thin and weak that "as the beams of an old shed stick out, so did my ribs stick out through little food." He decided that he needed strength and so he began to eat again. The ascetics were unhappy that he had ended his fast and left him in disgust.

Gautama attains enlightenment

Gautama spent six years trying to find enlightenment. He became disillusioned and thought he must be wasting his time. One day he was passing through a country called Maghada when he decided to have one last try. He sat down under the Bo tree (the Tree of Enlightenment) and concentrated his mind. He was determined not to stand up until he had found enlightenment.

On the morning of the Full Moon Day in May, he achieved a state of extreme peace that was free of the causes of human suffering. He had attained the spiritual truth he had been looking for, and so he became the Buddha, the "Enlightened One."

The Buddha begins preaching

The Buddha decided to preach about his enlightenment to the five ascetics who had left him. At first the ascetics did not want to listen to him, but soon they saw that he was different and wanted to know how he had achieved enlightenment. The Buddha preached his sermon to the ascetics in the Deer Park at Sarnath, near Varanasi.

The Buddha taught the ascetics the four "Noble Truths." He said that the world is full of suffering, and that the suffering was caused by human desires. Only if people set aside these desires could suffering end. The way to do this was to follow the "Eightfold Path." The

Fukukensaku Kannon is a female bodhisattva (one who has achieved nirvana), who is much revered.

FASCINATING FACTS

It is said that Gautama was born on the day of the full moon in May, and his birth was accompanied by earthquakes and thunder.
As soon as Gautama was born he took seven steps and said, "I am the chief in the world."

———— ❑ ————

Legends say that when Gautama left the comfortable life at home, he galloped out of the city on a horse, accompanied by gods. When he left his horse, it died of a broken heart and was reborn as a god.

———— ❑ ————

Today, a great temple stands on the spot where Gautama is said to have attained enlightenment. Pilgrims from all over the world visit the temple.

———— ❑ ————

Legends say that Gautama had to struggle with the evil tempter, Mara, who tried to persuade him to give up his search for spiritual truth and return to the comforts of his previous life. When Gautama overcame Mara, all the gods shouted for joy.

———— ❑ ————

People from every walk of life, rich and poor alike, loved the Buddha. One of his important converts was King Bimbisara of Rajagaha.

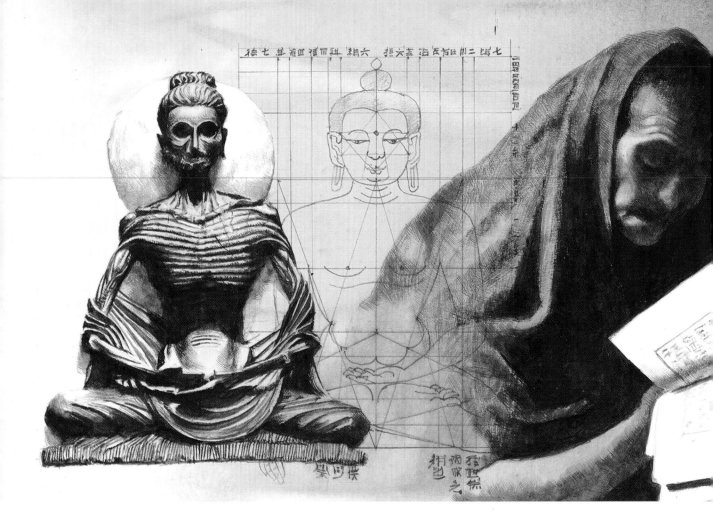

Path consists of things to do to ensure a good life, such as peaceful and pure conduct, telling the truth and being open, exercising self-control correctly, causing no injury, and meditating correctly on the meaning of life.

The first disciples

The five ascetics were inspired by the sermon and became the Buddha's disciples. As time went by, more people joined them and they lived together quietly, meditating during the rainy season and traveling from place to place teaching for the rest of the year.

During the Buddha's lifetime and for about 200 years after his death in about 480 B.C., his teaching only reached people in a small area of northeast India. It did not spread throughout India until the reign of King Asoka (Ah-SHOW-ka).

When Asoka came to the throne of the Mauryan Empire in 274 B.C., most of northern and central India had been united by his grandfather and father. Asoka managed to conquer the rest of India and added it to his empire. But he was so sickened by the cruelty of war that he converted to Buddhism and changed his way of life. It was then that Buddhism began to be spread widely, reaching nearby countries.

Asoka bans animal sacrifice

Asoka's views on the way people should behave were carved on pillars throughout his empire. One carving banned killing animals for sacrifice. Another said that people should lead good lives and respect their parents. Several mentioned new laws and one referred to the king himself. It read, "All men are my children."

Rival groups

More and more people adopted the Buddha's teachings and the way of life he advised. Missionaries were sent throughout the empire and into lands in the north and the jungles of Sri Lanka in the south. The "new" religion was liked because it welcomed anyone from anywhere.

As Buddhism spread, disagreements emerged and these arguments eventually split the religion into two groups. The Buddhists in the north were known as Mahayana Buddhists, and they called those in the south Hinayana Buddhists. (The word *yana* means "vehicle," *maha* means "great," and *hina* means "small.")

The Mahayana Buddhists considered that they were the "greater vehicle" who could save humankind, and called the Hinayana Buddhists the

Gautama spent six years attempting to find an answer to the world's sufferings. Eventually, he attained enlightenment under the Bo tree (a type of fig tree). The Buddha is usually portrayed as a teacher, but sometimes he is shown at the end of his fast or as an old man.

"lesser vehicle." But these Buddhists did not accept this name and called themselves Theravada Buddhists, which means "way of the elders."

Mahayana Buddhism spread in northwestern India, and then to China, Tibet, Korea, and Japan. The Theravada school spread from southern India into Sri Lanka, Burma, Thailand, and Southeast Asia.

Magnificent statues

The Buddha had always said that he was not a god, but simply a teacher who could show people the true way of life to follow. However, many legends have grown up about the Buddha, and many of his followers have regarded him as more than human.

He was usually portrayed by symbols, such as footprints or the tree under which he had found enlightenment. But the tradition grew of having images of the Buddha to meditate in front of, and magnificent statues of him began to appear in the temples. He is usually represented sitting cross-legged with one hand raised in blessing, although other images are also found.

After Asoka's death, the spread of Brahmanism, and later of Islam, led to the decline of Buddhism in India. Today, Theravada Buddhism is found in Sri Lanka, Burma, Cambodia, Thailand, and Laos. Mahayana Buddhism is mainly found in Vietnam, Japan, China, Tibet, and Korea.

Buddhism taught people how to live in peace and harmony, and its ideals survive throughout the world today.

Theravada monks shave their heads and wear yellow robes. Mahayana monks wear traditional red robes, and, in Tibet, they wear tall hats. Both groups carry alms bowls (dishes in which the monks collect food and gifts from local people). It is quite common in parts of Southeast Asia for a young man to spend a year or two as a monk before he starts work or gets married.

The Eightfold Path
The Eightfold Path consists of:
1 Right view – knowledge of the truth.
2 Right thought – the intention to resist evil.
3 Right speech – saying nothing that will hurt others.
4 Right action – respecting life, morality, and property.
5 Right livelihood – holding a job that does not injure others.
6 Right effort – striving to free one's mind from evil.
7 Right mindfulness – controlling one's feelings and thoughts.
8 Right concentration – practicing proper forms of concentration.

The Athenian Republic

Between 500 and 430 B.C., the city-state of Athens in Greece was the home of one of the most influential civilizations the world has ever seen. Scientists and mathematicians, playwrights and artists flourished as the citizens of Athens developed a unique form of government which they called demokratia. *Those seventy years inspired much of what we know as Western civilization.*

800   400   BC/AD   400   800   1200   1600   2000

c.450 BC Athens, Greece

The civilizations of the ancient world made many contributions to the way we live today. One of the most remarkable and impressive civilizations was that of ancient Greece. The Greeks left behind works of art which we can still marvel at. Philosophers, such as Socrates and Plato, changed the way people thought. Plays by Sophocles, Aristophanes and other playwrights are still performed. And the Greeks introduced a new form of government which is still followed in the modern world.

Ruthless rulers

People first settled in Greece about 8,000 years ago. Around 800 B.C., they had organized themselves into communities called city-states. Each city-state, or *polis* (from which we get the word "politics"), consisted of a walled

Pericles (c. 495–429 B.C.), the Athenian statesman who presided over Athens' golden age and organized the building of the Parthenon.

town or city surrounded by farm land. City-states were ruled by oligarchies – groups of powerful citizens – or by ruthless rulers called tyrants.

Beginnings of democracy

The people were unhappy about the way they were being ruled, and they began to demand a say in how their city-states were organized. Then, in about 500 B.C., a new form of government was introduced in Athens, which was the largest city-state. It was called *demokratia*, which means "government by the people" (the *demos*). (The English word "democracy" comes from this Greek word.)

All the citizens now had a say in how they were ruled and were allowed to vote for officials to take care of the day-to-day running of the city-state. Women and slaves were not counted as citizens,

which meant that only men were allowed to vote.

Every citizen was a member of the Assembly, where they could attend the weekly meetings and make their concerns known. Each year, a council of 500 officials was elected by drawing lots. The citizens also elected ten generals, who were responsible for protecting the city from invasion. The democratic system of government introduced in ancient Athens still forms the basis of politics two and a half thousand years later.

The Persian menace

The mighty Persian Empire was a constant threat to the city-states of Greece. Athens was plundered by the Persians in 480 B.C., and many of its buildings were destroyed. The city-states of Athens and Sparta managed to defeat the Persians at the Battle of Plataea in 479 B.C., but there were fears that they would try to invade again.

The Athenians suggested that all the city-states should join together to form an alliance, which was called the Delian League. Then, in 453 B.C., the Athenians moved all the league's money to a treasury in Athens. The league was turned into an Athenian empire, and the city became prosperous and powerful.

A city to marvel at

The flowering of Greece's golden age was largely due to a statesman called

Ancient Athens became the hub of Western civilization through the leadership of Pericles. Under his guidance, the magnificent temples, monuments and statues that still stand on the Acropolis – one of the high ridges that dominates modern Athens – were built.

Once a year, the members of the Athenian Assembly had a chance to exile any prominent citizen they disapproved of.

In 1806, sculptures from the Parthenon were taken to England by the Earl of Elgin. Known as the Elgin Marbles, the sculptures are in the British Museum, London. Many Greeks want the Marbles returned.

About 430 B.C., Democritus wrote down his theory of how the whole world is made up of atoms. He had to wait nearly 2,000 years before his theories were widely believed or tested.

About 500 B.C., the followers of Pythagoras, who was a great mathematician, taught that the Earth was a sphere and not saucer-shaped, as had been previously believed.

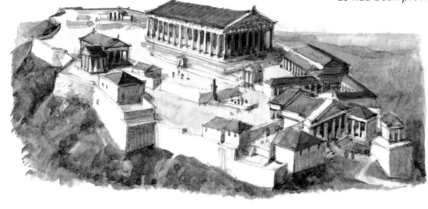

High on the rock of the Acropolis stood the Parthenon. The great temple was dedicated to the Greek goddess of wisdom, Athena, after whom the city of Athens was named.

Pericles. He was elected as the leader of the board of generals in 443 B.C., and this gave him the power to encourage artists, paid for by money from the Athenian treasury. People began to read and write and discuss ideas. This was the beginning of the age known as Athens' Classical Period.

Pericles wanted to create a beautiful new city that was the glory of Greece. Athens' greatest building is the Parthenon, a magnificent marble temple which was begun in 448 B.C. by the sculptor Phidias. It was built on the Acropolis, a rocky hill in the city, and it could be seen for many miles around.

Phidias carved marble statues and scenes on the stone walls to decorate the Parthenon. One was a 40 ft. (12m.) high statue of the goddess Athena in gold and ivory.

Playwrights and thinkers
One of the greatest Greek inventions was the theater. During the Classical Period, playwrights began to write the great tragedies – plays about unhappy events with a sad ending – and comedies, some of which still survive. The most famous writers of tragic plays were Aeschylus, Sophocles and Euripides. Aristophanes was the best-known writer of comedies.

This was also the period when philosophers, such as Socrates, Plato and Aristotle, began to question the way people saw the world, and how they thought and behaved. They began the exchange of ideas which is the basis of learning today.

The art of the the glorious Classical Period was copied by the Romans and later inspired the Renaissance in fourteenth-century Italy (see page 41).

Jesus Christ & Christianity

About 2,000 years ago, a Jew was crucified in an obscure corner of the Roman Empire. His inglorious death was unrecorded except by his followers. Yet from that death arose one of the great religions of Earth, based on the life of Jesus of Nazareth. More than one billion people around the world today follow versions of his teachings.

800   400   BC/   400   800   1200   1600   2000

c.32 AD Jerusalem, Israel

The life and death of Jesus Christ must be one of the greatest turning points in history. It may not have seemed so to people living at the time, however. During Jesus' lifetime, he had only a handful of followers. Some people listened to his preaching and marveled at his work. Others were his enemies, plotting his downfall. And more still had never heard of him.

From these beginnings stemmed the Christian religion which has spread throughout the world. It is estimated that there are nearly 950 million Christians, which is about a quarter of the world population. But the growth of Christianity did not happen overnight. It took hundreds of years.

The coming of a Messiah
Jesus was born in Judea, a small part of the mighty Roman Empire which stretched round

Jesus (c. 6 B.C.–C. A.D. 30). Many painters have tried to portray Jesus, but no one can be sure what he looked like.

the countries of the Mediterranean Sea and north into Europe. The early followers of Jesus practised Judaism, the religion of the Jews.

The Jews had long believed that a "Messiah," a descendant of King David, would come to save them from Roman rule. Jesus' followers believed that he was this Messiah. Jesus said that they were right to think he was the Messiah, but he said that he was not the earthly king they had been expecting. "My kingdom is not of this world," he said.

Miracles of healing
Jesus traveled through Galilee and Judea, teaching and performing miracles of healing. A group of followers, known as the twelve disciples, traveled and preached with him.

Jesus taught that the two great commandments were, "Love the Lord your God with all your heart" ... and "Love your neighbor as yourself."

The Jewish priests and scholars were unhappy with what Jesus preached, because he was challenging their authority. So Jesus was arrested by the guards of the Jewish High Priest and crucified on the orders of the Roman governor, Pontius Pilate.

Jesus rises from the dead

Jesus' opponents probably thought that once he was dead, his followers would disappear and forget the things he had said. They could not have been more wrong. Three days later, his followers were convinced that Jesus had came back to life. This wonderful event proved to them that Jesus really was the true son of God.

Many Christians met a cruel death in the Colosseum in Rome.

About six weeks after the crucifixion of Jesus, the disciples began to preach about his work and how he had been killed, but had risen from the dead. They started in Jerusalem, from where many converts set out to spread the word throughout the Roman Empire.

The priests were angry with the teachings of Jesus and the claims that he was the Messiah. They arranged his capture, trial and death on the cross. The Bible tells us that Jesus was buried in a stone tomb, but three days later the tomb was empty and he met the disciples again. Christians believe that Jesus died to save humankind from sin (wrongdoing), and that his rising from the dead proves that he was not merely a man, but the son of God.

The preachings of the disciples were still linked to Judaism, and followers lived by the rituals of the Torah, the holy book of the Jews. However, some of the preachers, such as Paul of Tarsus, began to move Christianity away from Judaism. They believed that this would attract more non-Jews to become Christians.

Thrown to the lions

The new faith soon spread as far as Rome itself. The Romans worshiped many gods, including the emperor who himself was seen as a god. But Christianity said that people should only worship the one true God and not men or idols. The Romans could not accept this, and thousands of Christians were killed or thrown into prison for their beliefs. Many were killed in public arenas, like the Colosseum in Rome, as part of the entertainment. Often they were given to lions or other wild animals, to be torn apart while spectators cheered.

The Roman historian Tacitus (c. A.D. 55–120) wrote about the Romans' behavior towards Christians during the

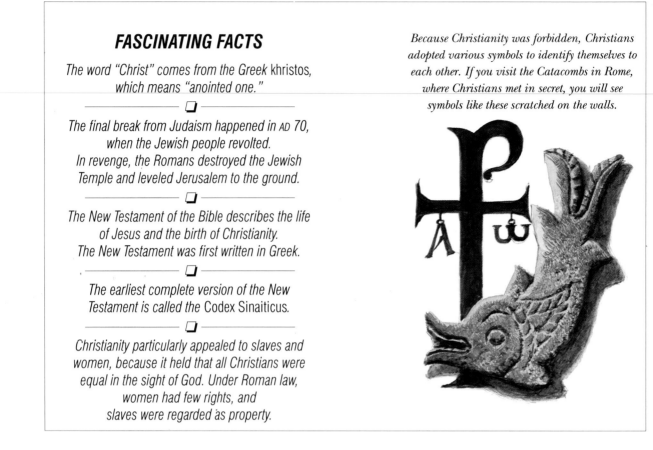
reign of the emperor Nero (reigned 54–68). His words show how suspicious the Romans were about these people who sought to put their God above the emperor. He wrote that the emperor had "charged and tortured some people hated for their evil practices – the group known as 'Christians.'"

The Byzantine emperors defended Christianity against the rise of Islam. They built churches and monasteries.

A Christian emperor

Rome continued to persecute the Christians, although not all the time. The Christians went on converting people in secret. About three hundred years after Christ's death, the Roman emperor Constantine the Great (c. 274–337) converted to Christianity and made it the religion of the empire in 324. This was a great step forward because it meant that Christians throughout the Roman world could now worship their God freely, and the Church could organize itself openly and spread its message.

Why did this new religion go from strength to strength? The answer probably lies in the cruelty of Christianity's opponents. The Christians did not fight back. They died for their faith, in the same way that Christ had done. Their witness to this new religion impressed people who were not convinced by the state religion or the "divine" emperors.

Muhammad & Islam

About 1,400 years ago, a new prophet appeared in Arabia. Inspired by visits from an angel, Muhammad set out to convert the world to the worship of the one god, Allah. Despite many setbacks, he united the Arab tribes and set them on the way to building a mighty empire which followed Islam. Today more than 840 million people follow the faith he preached.

| 800 | 400 | BC/AD | 400 | 800 | 1200 | 1600 | 2000 |

622 AD Mecca. Saudi Arabia

In the 7th century, the tribes who lived in Arabia were constantly fighting with each other, and so the country was unable to develop and prosper in any purposeful way. All that was changed by one man who founded a new religion, Islam. By A.D. 732 the warring Arabs had forged themselves into a powerful force and created an empire which stretched from West Africa to the Far East.

Prosperous city
The founder of the Islamic religion was Muhammad, the son of a merchant. He was born in A.D. 570 into the Quraysh tribe, which had settled near the prosperous city of Mecca. Mecca is about 60 miles (80 km) from the Red Sea, in what is now Saudi Arabia. Merchants traveled from the city and traded with Persia (now Iran), Yemen, Ethiopia, and the Roman Empire.

Muhammad (c. A.D. 570–632) was the Prophet and preacher of Islam. The Arabic writing above represents name of Allah, the one God.

Muhammad was brought up by foster parents since his mother and father were dead by the time he was 6 years old. At 24, he began to work for a rich, young widow, Khadija, and later married her.

Center of worship
At this time, the Arabs worshipped many different gods. One center of worship was an ancient shrine, the Kaaba, in Mecca. It was the custom among religious Arabs to spend one month in meditation on Mount Hira, near Mecca, each year. During Muhammad's visit in about 610, something happened to him which was to change the life of millions of people.

One night he was visited in his sleep by the angel Gabriel. The angel began to tell him about a new form of worship in

which there was only one God, Allah. Muhammad was to be the prophet of Allah and travel around converting people to his worship.

Muhammad was visited many more times by the angel who told him about the rituals and laws of Islam. These revelations were written down by Muhammad's companions in the years before he died. They form the Qur'an (or Koran), the holy book of Islam.

A new religion

Islam was a new religion, but it was also a continuation of Judaism and Christianity. Muhammad was said to be the last prophet after Adam, Noah, Abraham, Moses, and Jesus, who was seen as God's messenger rather than his son. So Muhammad began to preach in Mecca. He told people that he was not holy, but only Allah's messenger. He said that the people must worship the one God, Allah, and put aside evil ways before the end of the world, which was not far off.

The Hadith, which records traditions about the Prophet and his sayings, decrees that Muslims must pray five times a day and give charity each year to the poor. They must fast between dawn and sunset for one month, called Ramadan, and they must make a pilgrimage to Mecca, called the hajj.

Muhammad soon found followers, but his preaching did not please everyone. People already made pilgrimages to the Kaaba in Mecca, and

The Muslim place of worship is called a mosque. In Muslim countries, these buildings are often square with a dome. From a tall tower called a minaret, a man called a muezzin calls the people to pray five times a day. Muslim holy men are called ulamas, imams, or ayatollahs.

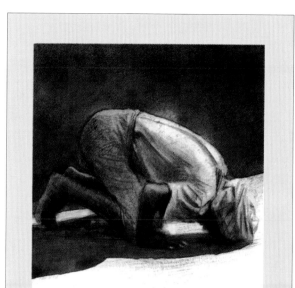

A Muslim at prayer.

FASCINATING FACTS

The word Islam is Arabic for "submission to the will of God," and its followers are Muslims. Muslim means "one who submits."

❏

Worshipers, wherever they are in the world, recite prayers facing towards Mecca in Saudi Arabia, the religious center of Islam. Muslims pray in different positions: standing, kneeling, and touching the ground with their foreheads.

❏

All Muslims must worship Allah five times a day in prayer. Before praying, people must wash to ensure that they are clean and pure.

❏

Once every year, Mecca is full of over a million Muslims who are there for the hajj. Muslims who have made the great pilgrimage are called hajji.

❏

Today, the main Muslim sects are the Sunnites and the Shiites. Shiites are mostly found in Syria, Iraq, and Iran.

❏

The Muslims developed a distinctive style of art and architecture which can be seen in the countries they conquered. Their buildings have domes and elaborate patterning. They are not allowed to make images of animals or humans.

this brought money and trade to the powerful merchants who ruled the city. They saw Muhammad as a threat and tried to drive him out by stoning him. In 622, Muhammad and his followers had to flee to Yathrib, about 300 miles (500 kilometers) to the north.

This flight, known as the hejira, was the turning point in the rise of Islam. Yathrib was soon renamed Medina, "the City of the Prophet," and the year 622 was later taken to be the start of the Muslim era.

to the city. He went to the Kaaba, the shrine of the old religion, and turned it into a shrine of Islam.

Islam stands for justice and for peace, but the Hadith says that force may be used against all those who are unjust to others. You will achieve paradise if you die fighting for Allah.

When Muhammad died in 632, he was planning a campaign into Roman territories in Palestine. His followers continued his work and appointed a caliph, or successor, to lead Islam. They began to build their empire. Over the next 300 years, the caliphs conquered Iraq, Syria, Egypt, and Persia.

By 661, their empire stretched from Tunisia in North Africa to the borders of India. The empire did not last, but the religion of Islam was established and millions of people continued to follow it. Today, over 840 million people around the world are Muslims.

The court of the caliph in Baghdad, Iraq.

Building an empire
Muhammad and his followers were safe in Medina, but Muhammad's work had only just begun. His first task was to defeat his old enemies in Mecca. He and his followers attacked caravans from Mecca – groups of merchants and travelers crossing the desert – as they passed on their trading journeys and also the pagan tribes.

Eight years after the hejira, a truce was agreed with Mecca, and in 629, Muhammad was welcomed back

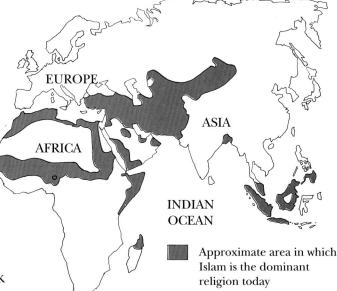

Approximate area in which Islam is the dominant religion today

Saints, Shepherds & Scholars

For nearly 500 years, what remained of the Greek and Roman civilizations was preserved by the monks and priests of the Christian church. They kept the manuscripts safe in the barbarian kingdoms of Europe and sent missionaries out to teach the tribes about Christianity and the rule of law. They colonized the wilderness and opened up new areas for peasant farmers to exploit.

800	400	BC/AD	400	800		1200	1600	2000

c.1100 Clairvaux, France

After the fall of the western Roman Empire in A.D. 476, there was a period known as the Dark Ages in Europe. The philosophy, art and literature that had flowered in Greek and Roman times was neglected. Instead, there was fighting between warring tribes. Europe was divided into small kingdoms ruled by invaders, barbarians who worshiped one or more non-Christian gods.

Christianity spreads
However, the popes in Rome were still head of the Christian church. Although less powerful than the barbarian king, they struggled to keep everything from being lost. For the next 500 years, Christian churchmen traveled around Europe, converting people to Christianity.

As Christianity spread, the barbarians began to adopt Roman ideas, such

St. Benedict of Nursia (c. A.D. 480–550) was a hermit before founding the first order of monks. He drew up his Rule so that his monks would know how to live a productive and holy life.

as the system of law and government, the art of writing and the Latin language. By the year 900, Christianity had been adopted in northwest Europe and was spreading eastwards and in Scandinavia. Monasteries were founded where monks withdrew from the world to pray and meditate. The monasteries also became centers of teaching, where people could learn to read and write, and study books written in Latin. The monasteries were a vital link in ending the Dark Ages.

Benedictine rules
The way in which the monasteries developed was due largely to one man, Benedict of Nursia. In 529, Benedict drew up a set of rules for monks which were later adopted by most monasteries. The Benedictines produced great scholars, like the Venerable Bede, who studied history,

Most orders of monks sang seven services every day.

theology and astronomy. Much of the monks' time was spent copying the illuminated manuscripts – books written by hand and decorated with colorful lettering and pictures – which were the only books available.

The monasteries were given large areas of land and became rich and powerful. Farming was the main source of wealth at this time, and landowners, including the abbots, wanted to increase their riches. Forests were cleared and land was drained to make new farm land.

The Cistercian monks played an important part in the clearance of

Most monasteries had a scriptorium – *a place where monks copied manuscripts and painted beautiful pictures in them – and a library. Many Greek and Roman works only survived because they were in a monastery library.*

land. The Cistercian order was founded in Citeaux in France in 1098. New monasteries were built in remote places and the monks combined working the land with their prayers.

Rebirth of art and learning
As the Dark Ages ended, there was a rebirth of art and learning. People began to ask questions about the link between Christianity and the thoughts of philosophers, such as Aristotle. The monasteries and later the cathedral schools were the only places where people could learn, but many students were eager to find out more.

In the twelfth century, cathedral schools began to attract more influential teachers who gathered scholars around them. Many European universities began as cathedral schools, like Paris, Padua and Oxford.

Marco Polo Travels to China

"Seeing this city for the first time, you might imagine yourself in Paradise," wrote Marco Polo describing one of the Great Khan's cities. His book about his extraordinary journeys and how he served Kublai Khan was thought to be all lies by many of his first readers. But merchants and statesmen read it too, and realized how little they really knew about the world....

| 800 | 400 | BC/AD | 400 | 800 | 1200 | 1600 | 2000 |

c.1290 Beijing, China

Before the days of the traveler, Marco Polo, the lands in the East were a mystery to people living in Europe. Marco Polo was not the first European to travel to China, but he was the first to write accounts of his journeys. He set up links between the East and West which have lasted to this day.

Rumors of a fabulous empire

Marco Polo (1254–1324) was the son of a merchant living in Venice. At this time, Venice was the trading capital of Europe. Merchant ships set out from the city to ports around the Mediterranean Sea and beyond.

Rumors had reached Europe about the fabulous Mongol Empire in the East. The huge empire stretched across much of eastern Europe and Asia, but the Mongol ruler, Kublai Khan, had his court in the city of

Kublai Khan (1215–94) was emperor of China for fifteen years. The grandson of Genghis Khan, he ruled China by the time of Marco Polo's journey.

Peking in China. The great Khan was feared as a mighty military leader, but little else was known about him at the time.

Venice's position in eastern Europe made it an ideal starting point for overland trading routes with the East. Among the first people to open up these routes were Marco Polo's father and uncle, Nicolò and Maffeo Polo. They spent a year at the court of the great Kublai Khan and found him to be a hospitable man with a great interest in the West. When the Polo brothers returned to Peking for a second time, Marco Polo went with them.

Marvelous sights

Marco was 17 when they set out in 1271; it was to be twenty years before he returned to Europe. During this time, he kept vivid records of his travels, including the difficult three-and-a-half year journey to China, when they had to cross the Gobi Desert.

But Marco's most interesting accounts are about the court of the great Khan. He described the magnificent palace with a hall that was so vast that 6,000 people could sit down to eat there. He told of prosperous cities, such as Hangchou, which he said was "beyond dispute the finest and noblest city in the world," and he described the famous Yangtze river as carrying "more wealth and merchandise than all the rivers and all the seas of Christendom put together."

Exaggerated accounts

Marco Polo was overwhelmed by what he found and his accounts were certainly exaggerated. Even so, his writings about the fabulous Chinese civilization enthralled people in the West. They were to remain the major authoritative works on the subject for centuries to come.

Marco Polo did not only explore China, but also traveled to other lands in the East, including Tibet, Burma and India, working for the Khan. All that Marco saw and studied was reported to the Khan and, because of his knowledge, Marco was able to give the Khan helpful advice.

Mongol rulers preferred to use foreigners in government posts rather than Chinese people, and Kublai Khan made Marco governor of Yangchow province, northeast of Nanking. His father and uncle were also employed by the Khan for sixteen years. But these foreign employees were kept apart from the local people, and even after seventeen years in China, Marco could hardly speak the language.

FASCINATING FACTS

After returning from China, Marco fought for the Venetians against the Genoese and was captured. In prison, he wrote an account of his travels which remained almost the only source of information about the Far East until the nineteenth century.

❑

Marco wrote of the New Year celebrations when the Khan received gifts of thousands of white horses, and 5,000 elephants appeared each carrying chests filled with the Khan's treasures.

❑

The Mongol or Yuan Dynasty ruled China from 1206 to 1368. In that year, the last Mongol emperor was overthrown by a Chinese uprising and a new dynasty began: the Ming.

❑

Marco found that coal was widely used in China. Coal was known in northern Europe, but was strange to him, coming from the southern city of Venice.

China was already known for its fine porcelain, and pieces had found their way to Europe. Some of the most beautiful was produced during the Ming Dynasty, like this blue and white porcelain flask.

Today, we take traveling all over the world for granted and few places hold much mystery. But in the Middle Ages large parts of the world were unexplored. Marco Polo traveled further than any other man of his time and brought back far more information.

The center of world trade

Marco Polo's journey established Venice as a world trading center. It was already linked to France, Germany, the Netherlands and the ports of the Mediterranean.

Now merchant ships began to arrive from the Far East, bringing carpets, silks and spices. The merchants of Venice became rich as they traded these goods across Europe. These links would probably have been established even if Marco Polo had not made his journeys. The Mongol Khans were interested in the West and realized that there was money to be made in trading.

But Marco Polo's travels created the links more quickly and established a greater understanding between East and West. He also paved the way for later travelers and explorers to follow in his footsteps and learn more about the "mysterious" world to the east.

The Venetian traveler, Marco Polo, was the first European to write an account of the Chinese empire. In China, Marco found a nation with a history thousands of years old. The rulers governed well, and there were many different religions existing at the same time without rivalry or fighting. Marco also saw people using paper money, which was a revelation to him. In many ways, the Chinese civilization was far ahead of that in Europe.

The Terror of the Black Death

In the 1340s, European merchants and rulers heard news of many people dying in Asia from a strange new disease. They shrugged this off – until the deaths started in their cities. That was the terror: people could catch this plague and die within 12 hours. Villages were wiped out; cities lost over half their population; farms were abandoned. No one knew who would be the next to go....

| 800 | 400 | BC/AD | 400 | 800 | 1200 | 1600 | 2000 |

1350 Europe

Trade routes between the East and West brought greater riches to merchants and opened up the world to travelers. But they also helped the spread of something far more sinister – the Black Death or bubonic plague.

The Black Death began in China in 1333. The disease was carried by fleas which lived on the bodies of animals, such as the black rat. Black rats traveled with merchants' caravans along trade routes, such as the Silk Road from China to Constantinople, Mecca, Baghdad and other cities of the Middle East.

Mysterious deaths

People in Europe had heard about the Black Death before it actually arrived. Rumors began to reach them about strange and tragic happenings far away in China. Millions of people were dying from some mysterious cause. The victims had black boils in their armpits and groins, and fever – a person who seemed perfectly well in the morning could be dead by the evening.

No one was safe

To the people of medieval Europe, anything that was happening in China must have seemed very far away – only a few merchants had ever visited the Far East – and they cannot have thought they were in any danger from these terrifying events. They could not know that the plague would kill twenty-five million people in Europe.

Why did the plague spread so suddenly? The rat may have been the first carrier of the disease, but infected

*The black rat (*Rattus rattus*) comes originally from Asia. They spread along the trade routes into Europe, traveling in ships and with merchant caravans, taking plague-carrying fleas with them.*

Most people died from some disease in medieval times. The horror of the plague brought death even closer.

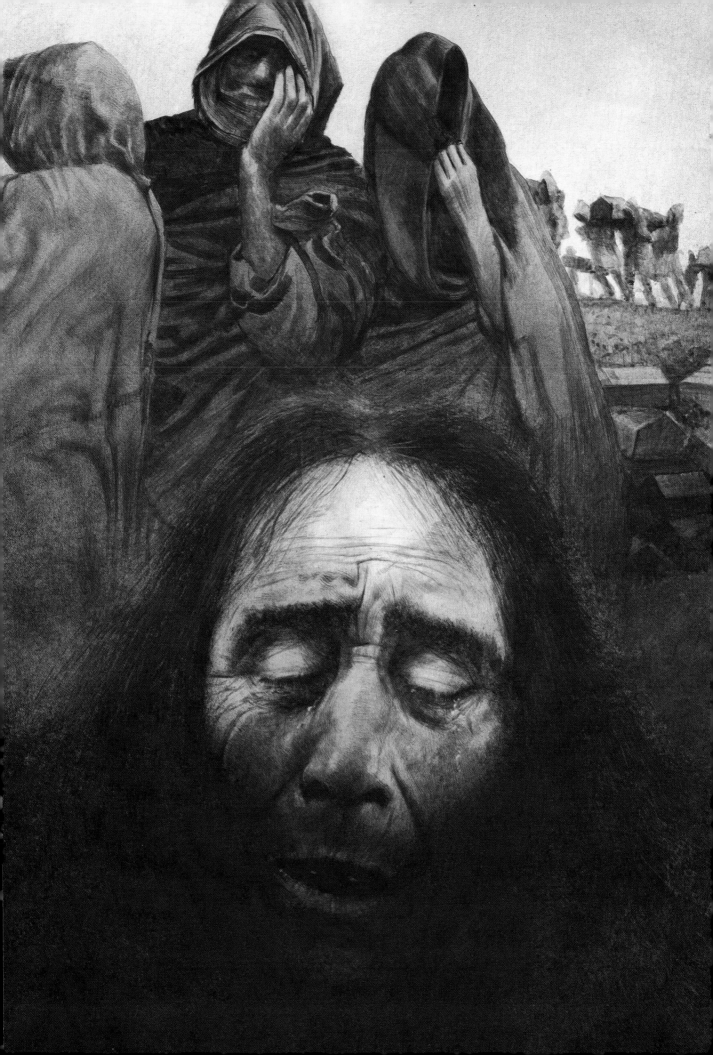

This cloaked figure was known as "the grim reaper," and represented Death. During the fourteenth century, Death also appears as a character in stories for the first time, and there was a fashion for putting skulls and skeletons on tombstones.

people soon began to pass it to others. The overland trade routes meant that people could move around far more quickly than before. Merchants and sailors on the shipping routes carried the plague by sea.

The disease reaches England

In 1346 Mongol soldiers attacked the city of Caffa on the Black Sea coast in the Crimea. Plague broke out among the Mongols and spread to the city. It reached Europe through Caffa's trading routes with the Mediterranean. By 1348, the disease had reached France and England.

The effects of the plague in Europe were devastating – whole towns were wiped out. When the plague had passed, there was more food for those who were left and so the life of poor people improved a little.

The main turning point, however, was that there was a shortage of people to work the land and so labor was in demand. Before the plague, the "feudal system" had been in operation. Rich landowners gave poor people a plot of land to work. In return, the people had to serve their landlord and also fight for him in times of war. Many landlords were harsh and cruel masters. But people were now able to take advantage of all the land which was available and the feudal system began to disappear.

There was also a religious revival because people believed that the plague was God's punishment for wrongdoings. So the plague had an important influence in the way medieval life was organized.

The Medicis & the Renaissance

Even as the Black Death raged through Europe, artists, writers and scholars in the city-states of Italy began to point Western culture onto a new track. Inspired by the arts of ancient Greece and Rome, they invented new ways of painting, new forms of poetry, new ways of looking at the world. The fabulously wealthy merchant-rulers of Florence, the Medicis, supported this "rebirth."

| 800 | 400 | BC/AD | 400 | 800 | 1200 | 1600 | 2000 |

1470 Florence, Italy

In the middle of the fourteenth century, a glorious new age began in Europe. It brought about changes that were so far-reaching that it was given a special name – the Renaissance, or "rebirth" of Europe.

Accepted ideas challenged

The Renaissance marks the end of the Middle Ages and the start of modern thought. During the Middle Ages, most people had been happy to accept ideas handed down by such authorities as the church. In the Renaissance, people began to challenge the accepted ideas, and this led to new discoveries that were to have an enormous impact on the world.

Established thought had already been questioned in the twelfth century by the French philosopher, Peter

Lorenzo the Magnificent (1449–92) was so interested in the arts that he neglected the family business and the Medicis began to lose their wealth.

Abelard (1079–1142), who angered many people by challenging some of the statements in the Bible. During the thirteenth century, more and more people became interested in the art and literature of ancient Greece and Rome. When the Byzantine empire began to fall to the Turks in the mid-fourteenth century, Greek scholars fled to Italy. It was here that the Renaissance began.

Ruling families

Italy was divided into city-states ruled by wealthy families. The principal city of the Renaissance was Florence, which was ruled over by the Medicis. The Medicis were a noble family that had become rich and powerful through trading and business in Italy and the rest of Europe, and they spent

their wealth on creating a beautiful city full of works of art.

The Medicis' power was established by Cosimo de' Medici (1389–1464), who also began the tradition of supporting artists by giving them money. Brunelleschi and Donatello were two famous artists employed by Cosimo. It was due largely to Cosimo that Florence was the most famous city for Renaissance art and learning.

Another great Medici was Lorenzo the Magnificent(1449–92), who supported the outstanding artists, Botticelli and Michelangelo.

However, the Medicis were not always noble in their actions. For, although they loved beautiful things, they also loved to rule and enjoyed power. Lorenzo, for example, kept many spies, schemed and used violence in an attempt to defeat his rivals. He earned his title of "the Magnificent" for the books, paintings

and sculptures in his palace, and not for the way he exercised his power.

Niccolò Machiavelli was a writer and politician in Florence during the Medicis' rule. He was dismissed by the Medicis in 1512 and wrote his famous work, *The Prince*, in which he said that a ruler must use any means, however cruel and unscrupulous, to keep power. Today, we still use the word "Machiavellian" to describe someone who is devious and cunning.

People all round the world remember the Renaissance for the magnificent works of art of the period, and for the impressive churches and palaces that were decorated with paintings and statues by the great artists of the day. However, many scientific discoveries were made during this period, too. Paracelsus, a Swiss, made important medical discoveries, and the Polish astronomer, Nicolaus Copernicus, discovered proof that the Earth and all the other planets moved around the sun.

Inventions and artists

One important change brought about by the Renaissance was the style of painting. The paintings of the Middle Ages looked flat and not at all like the world as we see it, whereas the paintings of the Renaissance artists looked more lifelike. The Renaissance artists introduced perspective, which gave a sense of distance like that in real life. They studied the human body and used living models for their work, so the people in their paintings looked like real people.

The men and women of the Renaissance did not stick to one area of interest only. For example, Leonardo da Vinci was a painter, sculptor, philosopher, engineer and scientist. He designed a flying machine (this was never built), and also a "covered car, safe and unassailable" for use in war. This was the tank, which he pictured 400 years before tanks were actually built for battle. Leonardo also made detailed studies of the human body and was a mathematician.

The printing press was invented during this time. Printing was already known in China, but was unknown in Europe until Johannes Gutenberg, from Mainz in Germany, invented printing with movable type. He printed his first book, the Bible, in 1456.

Michelangelo is best known for his sculpture and his paintings on the ceiling of the Sistine Chapel in Rome. But he was also a poet and philosopher, and the architect of St. Peter's in Rome. Today, people still flock to see the work of these and other artists of the Renaissance.

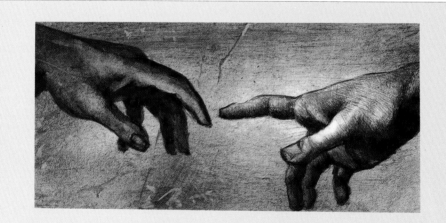

Detail from "The Creation of Man" in the Sistine Chapel, painted by Michelangelo.

FASCINATING FACTS

Cesare Borgia belonged to one of the noble ruling families of Rome and was a son of Pope Alexander VI. He is chiefly remembered for his murders and treachery. His sister, Lucrezia, has an undeserved reputation for vice and crime.

The dome of Florence Cathedral, built by Brunelleschi, was the largest since the Pantheon of ancient Rome. Brunelleschi used bands of stone to support the dome, instead of the huge framework of scaffolding used in earlier times.

Visitors to Florence can see Giotto's Campanile (Bell Tower) and the Ponte Vecchio, a bridge lined with shops across the River Arno.

Cosimo de' Medici the Great (1519–74) collected Etruscan antiques. The Etruscans ruled most of Italy before the rise of Rome.

Columbus Lands in America

On August 3, 1492, three tiny ships set sail from Palos in Spain. Led by an ex-pirate, they headed westwards into the Atlantic looking for a sea route to China. What they found instead was America – a "new world" lying ready for conquest. The courage and determination that Columbus needed to strike out across the mighty ocean make this one of the greatest feats of exploration ever.

| 800 | 400 | BC/AD | 400 | 800 | 1200 | | 1600 | 2000 |

1492 San Domingo

The fifteenth century was a particular turning point in history. It was one of the great ages of European exploration and expansion. Europeans crossed the Equator for the first time. Bartholomeu Dias sailed round the Cape of Good Hope at the southern tip of Africa. Vasco da Gama found a route to India round the Cape of Good Hope. And Christopher Columbus sailed the Atlantic and found America.

Earlier explorations
Columbus did not actually discover America. Others, such as the Vikings, had landed there far earlier, but they only explored a small corner in the north of the continent. Until Columbus arrived in the West Indies in 1492, no one had any idea there was a vast mass of land between Europe and Asia.

Before this time, the Chinese led the way in

Christopher Columbus (1451–1506) was born in Genoa, Italy and first went to sea at the age of 8. He was a pirate for a while, before going to Portugal in 1476.

exploring the world, and they made many rich and valuable trading friends. For example, the Chinese admiral, Cheng Ho, sailed his huge fleet of junks – flat-bottomed sailing ships – all over the eastern oceans, into the Indian Ocean and round the Cape of Good Hope. Then suddenly he turned his ships round and went home. He did not try to go further afield than the African coast, leaving it to the Europeans to sail across vast, unknown stretches of ocean and open up new sea routes.

Chinese puzzle
Cheng Ho's fleet was larger and his ships stronger than anything the Europeans had. So why did he not explore even further away from home?
The answer lies in the fact that China was rich and had many trading links. The country was stable and peaceful, and

so it did not need to open up new trade routes or conquer new lands.

Europe, on the other hand, was relatively poor and needed the gold and spices that came from the East. It was also under threat of war from the Turks, who had conquered much of the Middle East and were moving west. Europe was divided into many weak states who were often quarreling with each other. They had trade links with the East, but the routes were long and difficult, and often through enemy territory. The only way out of the situation seemed to be to find new sea routes to the East.

Columbus leads the way

Christopher Columbus was born in the Italian city of Genoa in 1451. Genoa had one of the largest fleets in the Mediterranean. The city traded with the East, but the ships needed a free passage through the eastern

The coat of arms granted to Columbus by Ferdinand and Isabella of Spain. In addition, he gained the right to call himself Admiral of the Ocean Sea.

Christopher Columbus set sail from Palos with three ships: the Santa Maria, *the* Niña *and the* Pinta. *His idea was to find a trading route by sea to bring back fabulous silks, spices and other goods from the East by traveling westwards. The* Santa Maria *was about 70 ft. (21.2 meters) long, while the* Niña *and the* Pinta *were much smaller. It is not surprising that the crews were nervous about the voyage, setting off into the unknown on such tiny ships.*

Mediterranean and into the Black Sea. When the Turks captured Constantinople in 1453, they closed the route into the Black Sea.

At this time, Portugal was one of Europe's great sea powers. Columbus could see that there was now no future with the Genoese fleet and so he went to Lisbon to sail on Portuguese ships.

Columbus wanted to find a new route to the East. He had read the writings of Marco Polo which described the long journey from Europe to China. So Columbus reasoned that it must be a shorter distance to travel in the other direction, to the west. The problem was that Marco Polo had greatly exaggerated the distance to China. And Columbus thought the world was much smaller than it actually is. So the task he set himself was impossible – he could never have reached China by sailing west as his crew would have

Month symbols from the Mayan calendar. This civilization of Central America had a more accurate calendar than Europe.

By 1492, Columbus had three ships for the adventure. His flagship, the *Santa Maria*, had a crew of fifty men. The other two ships, the *Pinta* and *Niña*, were smaller with crews of thirty and twenty-four men.

Columbus sets sail

The ships sailed from the port of Palos on August 3 and reached the Canary Islands five days later. From there they set out to cross the Atlantic Ocean. The men were uneasy as day after day passed without sighting land. There were several false sightings which raised the sailors' hopes and then made them even more unhappy. Columbus had to reassure the crew and persuade them to carry on with the journey.

At last they really did see land. It was October 12, 1492 and they had arrived at an island which Columbus called San Salvador. He thought that he had reached an island on the eastern edge of Asia. The distances seemed to fit the maps and his idea of the world's size. In fact, he had arrived in the Bahamas, at what is now called Watling Island. He and his crew were greeted by the native people who were mystified by their strange visitors.

died from thirst and hunger first.

Of course, Columbus did not know all this when he began to plan his expedition. His main problem was finding someone to support him in the venture. Genoa and Portugal both refused to help him. But Spain wanted to compete with Portugal in exploration and trading, and so the king and queen of Spain, Ferdinand and Isabella, agreed to support Columbus.

The search for gold

Columbus visited other islands in the Bahamas. The inhabitants were friendly and told the sailors that there was gold on one of the West Indian islands, Cuba. Columbus set off at once, thinking this must be Japan. He could find little gold on Cuba, but the people told him about a large continent beyond, where a fierce people, the Caribs, lived. Columbus thought these Caribs must be Chinese pirates. His supplies were running low so he decided to return to Spain to report what he had found. First, he sailed to modern-day Haiti, in the Caribbean, which he named Hispaniola.

The *Santa Maria* is lost

Now disaster struck. The *Santa Maria* ran aground on the rocky coast of Hispaniola. Columbus managed to save his crew and supplies, but he could not save his ship. The sailors transferred to the other two ships and set sail for Spain.

Columbus arrived in triumph to be greeted by the king of Portugal and Ferdinand and Isabella of Spain. This was the start of a new era, when many explorers and adventurers would follow Columbus across the Atlantic, and shiploads of people would set out to settle in what was now known as the "New World." (Columbus himself returned to the New World three times. He returned ill after his third voyage and died not long afterwards.)

Great riches

People began to settle in Panama in 1519, then Mexico, Peru, Guatemala and central Chile. First, the Spaniards had to conquer the native peoples who lived there, such as the Aztecs of Mexico and the Incas of Peru. They found a great wealth of precious metals and other valuable items, which they exported to Spain. Spain collected great riches and also began an influence over Central and South America which has remained to the present day.

FASCINATING FACTS

The first explorers to reach America called the people they found there Indians because they thought they had reached India. In fact, these people had crossed a "land bridge" from Siberia to Alaska about 25,000 years earlier and settled in different parts of America.

❏

Columbus made three more voyages to the New World, discovering Guadeloupe, Puerto Rico, Jamaica, Trinidad and the mainland of South America.

❏

On his second voyage, Columbus founded the first town in the New World, which he named Isabella after the queen of Spain. It is now a ruin in the Dominican Republic.

❏

Columbus' third voyage ended in disaster. There was a revolt against his command and he was sent back to Spain in chains.

This stone-bladed knife was used for human sacrifices. The priests would cut open the victim's chest and offer his heart to the sun god.

A skull relief from the Ball Court at Chichen Itza in Mexico.

Luther & the Protestants

As a priest, Martin Luther condemned corruption wherever he saw it. When he found it in his own church, he spoke out against it despite the risk to his own life. He and his followers, called Protestants because they protested about these evils, broke away from the Pope and Rome to cause a split among Christians that has lasted until today.

800	400	BC/AD	400	800	1200	1600	2000

1517 Wittenberg, Germany

By the end of the fifteenth century, the popes who governed the Roman Catholic church from Rome had become powerful and rich. Even emperors and kings bowed to their authority.

The Pope and priests told people that they could buy "indulgences" by giving money to the church. This would ensure that they were not punished in the next world. Many people believed this, and the clergy became very wealthy.

But some people were beginning to question the practices of the Roman Catholic church and to criticize the power it had. This rebellion was to bring about a movement to reform the church and led to the establishment of a new church – the Protestant church. One man stands out above all others as the leader of what is called the

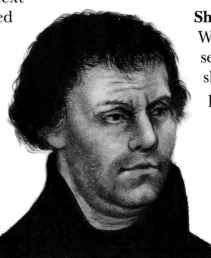

Martin Luther (1483–1546) criticized the Roman Catholic church after seeing a monk selling "indulgences" – forgiveness for their sins – to people in Rome.

Reformation. His name was Martin Luther.

Luther was the son of a miner in Saxony, a province in what is now Germany. He studied at the University of Erfurt and then became a monk. In 1511 he became a professor of theology – a teacher who studies God and the duty people have to Him – at Wittenberg.

Shocking scenes

When Luther saw people selling indulgences, he was shocked. He believed that people could only be forgiven for their sins by repenting, not by giving money to the Pope.

Luther set out his views in a statement of ninety-five beliefs, his *Treatise on Indulgences*. In 1517, as a defiance, he nailed a copy of it to the door of the Wittenberg Castle chapel. He also sent copies of the *Treatise* to

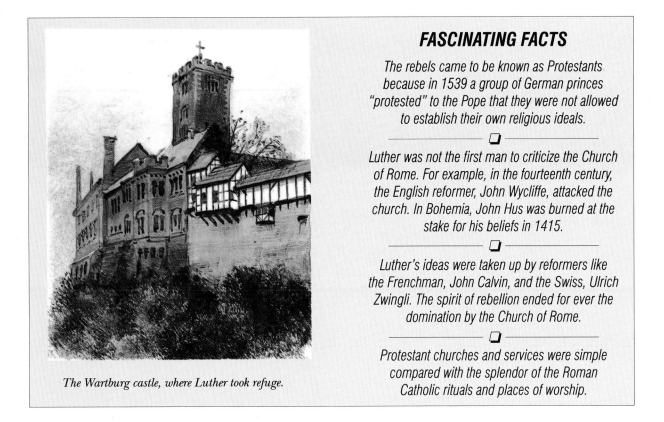

The Wartburg castle, where Luther took refuge.

many important clergymen.

Luther's statement went much further than a criticism of the behavior of the clergy. He believed that people should have faith in God and not rely on the priests – their influence should be reduced and people should follow the teachings of the Bible.

Some people were horrified by Luther's opinions. The priests saw that if his ideas were adopted, it would be the end of the church as they knew it. Others welcomed the statement. The artist Albrecht Dürer claimed that Luther was only saying what everyone else thought. The Pope threatened to excommunicate Luther (or throw him out of the church) if he did not take back what he had said. He refused and was excommunicated the next year.

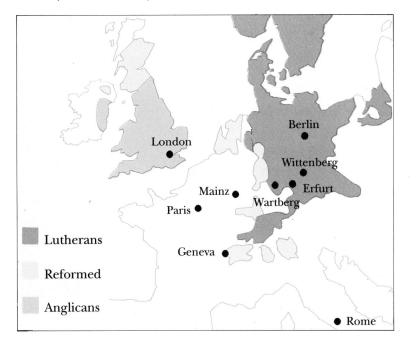

By 1600, there were Protestants in many parts of Europe.

In 1521, the Holy Roman Emperor, Charles V, summoned Luther to a Diet (special meeting) at Worms, a city in Germany, where he was again asked to change his views. Again Luther refused. The emperor issued the Edict of Worms which declared that Luther was an outlaw of the land. He was forced to leave the empire and his writings were burned.

Frederick of Saxony offered Luther refuge at his castle at Wartburg. While he was staying there, Luther began his translation of the Bible into German, which took him ten years to complete.

By this time, Luther's views were supported by a large number of people. The invention of printing helped the spread of his ideas. By the time he was banned in 1521, the books and pamphlets he had written had spread right across Europe.

The result of the Reformation
The Reformation began religious divisions which have continued to this day. Luther's belief that the scriptures were the only real source of truth led to a closer study of the Bible. This in turn led to translations of the Bible from Latin (a language which only the clergy and well-educated could then understand) into most European languages by the end of the century. Ordinary people could now study the teachings of the Bible for themselves.

While in exile in Wartburg castle, Luther continued to write and preach about his views. About fifty out of the eighty-five major cities of Europe joined the Reformation. Monks traveled around preaching about Luther's ideas, and so the Reformation spread to small towns and villages that books did not reach.

Magellan Circles the World

In August 1522, a battered ship loaded with cloves and spices limped into the port of Sanlucar de Barrameda in Spain. It had come a long way with that cargo, but its achievement was much more than a commercial success. It was Magellan's flagship, the Victoria, and it was the first ship ever to sail around the world. It was living proof that the world is round.

| 800 | 400 | BC/AD | 400 | 800 | 1200 | | 1600 | 2000 |

1521 Magellan Straits, Chile

Magellan's voyage to sail around the world came during a great age of exploration in the fourteenth and fifteenth centuries. Magellan was born in 1480 in northern Portugal. He went to sea as a young man and by the time he was in his thirties, he had proved himself a courageous sailor.

in South America. Magellan tried to persuade the king of Portugal to back him in an expedition. The king was not interested, so Magellan turned to King Charles V of Spain for help. He agreed to help him, and in 1517 Magellan signed papers making him a Spanish citizen.

New trade routes

Finding new trade routes was important for the countries of Europe, and Magellan thought he knew of a westerly route to the Spice Islands (the Moluccas) – a group of islands between Southeast Asia and Australia. He had studied the latest maps very carefully and talked to the Portuguese map-maker, Rui Faleiro. Faleiro thought it would be possible to sail from the Atlantic Ocean to the Pacific Ocean through a narrow strait

Ferdinand Magellan (1480–1521) undertook many voyages to India and Africa before setting out on the epic journey that was to lead to his death.

Magellan sets sail

Magellan spent two years preparing for his voyage. Charles V gave him five ships, but they were old and needed repairs to make them strong enough for such a long voyage. Magellan loaded his ships with dried and salted food, and with cloth, knives, mirrors and glass beads which they planned to trade for spices.

The ships set sail on September 20, 1519. They sailed across the Atlantic and reached

Brazil in December. After resting in Rio de Janeiro, they sailed south and reached San Julian Bay by the end of March 1520. The weather was bitterly cold, so Magellan decided to spend the winter here.

A mutiny is planned

There were no supplies of fresh food and the sailors became hungry. Some of them planned a mutiny, but Magellan managed to put a stop to this, and in June the ships were ready to set sail again.

On October 21, 1520, Magellan found the stretch of water that would take him through to the Pacific. (He named the land on his left-hand side Tierra del Fuego, which means "land of fire," because of the many fires that could be seen burning ashore.)

His method was to send one or two ships on ahead to explore the coast and report back. First he sent the smallest ship, the *Santiago*. The crew failed to find the strait and the ship was wrecked. In October, he sent two other ships, the *Concepcion* and the *San Antonio*. They returned to say that they had found a route. But the crew of the *San Antonio* were unhappy with the voyage. They took over their ship and sailed for home.

A way through

The rest of the ships went on through the strait, which they named the Strait of Magellan. The rough conditions were hazardous for such small ships, and the journey took thirty-eight days. At last they reached the Pacific Ocean on November 28. (Pacific means peaceful – Magellan found gentle and steady winds there and the water was not very rough.)

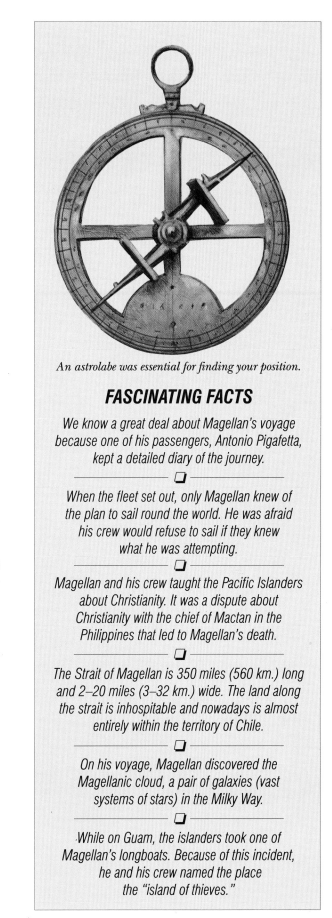

An astrolabe was essential for finding your position.

FASCINATING FACTS

We know a great deal about Magellan's voyage because one of his passengers, Antonio Pigafetta, kept a detailed diary of the journey.

❏

When the fleet set out, only Magellan knew of the plan to sail round the world. He was afraid his crew would refuse to sail if they knew what he was attempting.

❏

Magellan and his crew taught the Pacific Islanders about Christianity. It was a dispute about Christianity with the chief of Mactan in the Philippines that led to Magellan's death.

❏

The Strait of Magellan is 350 miles (560 km.) long and 2–20 miles (3–32 km.) wide. The land along the strait is inhospitable and nowadays is almost entirely within the territory of Chile.

❏

On his voyage, Magellan discovered the Magellanic cloud, a pair of galaxies (vast systems of stars) in the Milky Way.

❏

While on Guam, the islanders took one of Magellan's longboats. Because of this incident, he and his crew named the place the "island of thieves."

Ferdinand Magellan was the first person to cross the Pacific Ocean from the east to west. He is famous for discovering the Strait of Magellan, and also because his flagship for the voyage was to be the first to sail round the world. Magellan was killed in a fight with the natives of the Philippine Islands and so did not complete the adventure.

Now the water was calmer and the ships could make better progress. But Magellan did not know how far he still had to go to reach land. The supplies of food ran out, and the crew had to chew on leather straps and eat stewed rats to stay alive.

On March 6, 1521, the little fleet finally reached the first of the Pacific Islands, Guam. Here at last, they could anchor and find fresh food. The ships sailed on among the islands. In April, they arrived at the Philippine island of Mactan. Here they became involved in a fight with the local chief and a fierce battle raged. Magellan fought bravely to defend his men, but he and forty of his crew were killed. The rest of the crew continued to the Moluccas Islands, filled the ships with spices and struggled home. One of the ships, the *Trinidad*, was so badly battered that it had to be abandoned. Now only the flagship, the *Victoria* was left. About three years after the start of the voyage, the *Victoria* arrived home alone. Only eighteen of the original crew were on board.

Magellan's achievement

Although Magellan did not live to complete his voyage, it was his courage and determination that kept the fleet going through all the hazards they encountered. The historian Samuel Eliot Morrison summed up his achievement, when he wrote that Magellan crossed the difficult waters of the Atlantic "and overcame mutiny, starvation and treachery to cross the Pacific Ocean, which he named." The survivors in his party saw to it that the voyage was completed so that the "two halves" of the world were finally linked.

Right The islands of the Pacific Ocean provided a welcome opportunity for Magellan and his men to rest and load up the ships with food. The bananas, coconuts and other fruit would have relieved the cases of scurvy (a disease caused by a lack of fresh fruit and vegetables) among the sailors. The spices that the travelers traded for — like cinnamon, cloves, turmeric or nutmeg — would fetch a very high price in Europe.

Mayflower Sails for America

On November 20, 1620, a shivering group stood on the foreshore of a bay in what is now the state of Massachusetts. They had survived the dreadful Atlantic storms, pirates, sickness and religious persecution. They had reached their "Promised Land" where they – the Pilgrim Fathers – would build a new kind of state, based on their religious ideals.

| 800 | 400 | BC/AD | 400 | 800 | 1200 | 1600 | 2000 |

1620 Plymouth, Massachusetts, USA

In 1620 a small ship called the *Mayflower* set sail from Plymouth, England. On board were 102 people who were crossing the Atlantic Ocean to begin a new life in North America.

First colonies

The first people from Europe to colonize (settle in) America went to an area known as Virginia (now called North Carolina). The colonies had been founded by Sir Walter Raleigh in the 1580s, and the people who lived there hoped to earn their fortune from trading goods. However, they were not successful – only one settlement, Jamestown, survived.

The people who sailed on the *Mayflower* were not interested in becoming rich. Many were religious people who wanted a place to settle where they could be free to worship God in their own way.

Some of the new settlers were Puritans. They were a group of Christians who hated anything to do with the Roman Catholic church. The Puritans were not liked in England, because they were too strict in their beliefs for most people.

John Winthrop (1588–1649) was an able leader who, with other settlers, paved the way to the formation of the region known as New England.

Starting again

The settlers did not know what dangers the unknown land would hold. But they thought that the only way to be free was to start afresh in the new country. Life was hard in England in many ways – half the people were poor and had nowhere to live, and there was not enough work or food for everyone – and this made their decision to leave England easier.

Survival in a new land

On its journey to North America, the *Mayflower* was blown off course. Instead of landing in Virginia, the ship landed further north in what is now Massachusetts. The settlers called their landing place Plymouth, after the port they had sailed from.

It was winter and they had to find shelter and food if they were to survive. They built houses from wood and other materials they found nearby, but they did not know which plants were suitable for growing as food. They learned what they could from the native tribes, and produced food as best they could.

There were no laws to live by in the new land, and so the settlers made up their own. They lived by themselves until more settlers arrived from England ten years later. A

The Mayflower *on its journey to America.*

company called "The company of Massachusetts Bay in New England" wanted to trade with the settlers in North America. It was led by a man called John Winthrop.

The new wave of settlers

In 1629, some settlers from Winthrop's company founded the town of Salem just north of Plymouth. The following year, Winthrop set sail with a fleet of ships carrying a thousand men and women. They settled on the Charles River and founded a town they called Boston.

Winthrop was a Puritan and was glad to leave England. Like the *Mayflower*, his fleet arrived in winter, and the people had to struggle to find food and shelter. But the settlers of Plymouth were able to help them and soon the newcomers began to prosper.

FASCINATING FACTS

When the settlers arrived in the new land, they found many tribes of people living there. The Native Americans were the descendants of people who had crossed the land bridge from Asia (now the Bering Strait) thousands of years earlier. Each tribe had its own language and way of life.

❑

The colonists formed communities based on religion. Land was given to newly arrived groups of people. Each group agreed to build a church on their land. The church members then divided up the land among the individual families.

New England was named by Captain John Smith (c. 1580–1631), who was one of the early colonists. The area includes the six northeastern states of the U.S.: Connecticut, Rhode Island, Maine, Massachusetts, New Hampshire and Vermont.

❑

Today, Plymouth in Massachusetts has a population of about 45,600. Its industries include fishing and tourism. Boston is the capital of Massachusetts and has a population of about 575,000.

On November 21, 1620, after sixty-six days at sea, the Mayflower *reached North America. It was a hard winter with little food and much illness. Many of the group died, but those that survived built a settlement they called Plymouth. By November 1621, their first crops were harvested, and they gave thanks to God in a dinner that has become Thanksgiving – a special holiday in the U.S. and Canada which is celebrated with prayers and feasting.*

More colonists began to arrive from England and, by 1640, about 14,000 people had settled in the area. By the end of the seventeenth century, there were British colonies in Maine, New Hampshire, Maryland, Carolina and Pennsylvania.

The Puritans left England because they were not allowed to behave as they wished. The value they put on personal freedom attracted many people from Europe to North America, and laid the foundation for later settlers to build on.

The *Mayflower* compact

This agreement was drawn up by the Pilgrim Fathers on the *Mayflower* by which they planned to govern themselves in the new land.

In the Name of God, Amen. We, whose names are underwritten, the Loyal Subjects of our dread Sovereign Lord King James, by the Grace of God, of Great Britain, France, and Ireland, King, Defender of the Faith, etc. Having undertaken for the Glory of God, and Advancement of the Christian faith, and the Honour of our King and Country, a voyage to plant the first colony in the northern Parts of Virginia; Do by these Presents, solemnly and mutually in the presence of God and one another, covenant and combine ourselves together into a civil Body Politick, for our better Ordering and Preservation, and Furtherance of the Ends aforesaid; And by Virtue hereof do enact, constitute, and frame, such and equal Laws, Ordinances, Acts, Constitutions, and Offices, from time to time, as shall be thought most meet and convenient for the general Good of the Colony; unto which we promise all due Submission and Obedience.

Captain Cook's Voyages

"Land Ho!" came a cry from the lookout perched high above the heaving deck. Officers and men alike of HMS Endeavour ran out to get their first sight of this unknown continent. Once on land, although they did not find the dragons and monsters of earlier mapmakers, they did discover extraordinary animals ranging from koala bears to kangaroos. They had found – Australia.

800	400	BC/AD	400	800	1200	1600	2000

1770 Botany Bay, NSW, Australia

No man charted so much of the globe as the British explorer, Captain James Cook. He made three major voyages between 1768 and 1779, during which he mapped the Pacific islands, New Zealand and the east coast of Australia. Cook also claimed Australia for Britain, an event that was to play a large part in shaping Australia's history.

First command

Cook was born in 1728, the son of a farm worker from Yorkshire in England. When he was 18, he went to sea as an apprentice and soon became master of his own merchant ship. He joined the Royal Navy and after only two years, he was given command of his first ship, HMS *Pembroke*. Later, Cook served in Canada where he mapped difficult waters and began to establish his reputation

Captain James Cook (1728–79) charted the southern hemisphere and was awarded a medal for his work which put an end to scurvy among sailors.

as a skilled navigator.

At this time British scientists were taking a great interest in astronomy: the study of the stars and planets. In June 1769, the planet Venus was due to pass between the Earth and the sun. Cook had seen a similar eclipse of the sun when he was in the North Atlantic. Because of this and his skill with maps, he was chosen to lead an expedition to the Pacific island of Tahiti to report on the event. Cook was given a ship, the *Endeavour*, and a crew of ninety-seven men. A group of scientists sailed with them.

The ship set sail in August 1768 and landed

The Endeavour *was a converted coal ship. It was solidly built, which meant it could withstand the rough seas that Cook was to encounter on the long journey first to the Pacific and then Australia.*

One reason for the journey was to improve navigation. Cook used scientific instruments and nautical tables to pinpoint his position and produce accurate maps.

on Tahiti in time for the team of scientists to watch the eclipse. Cook and his officers then decided to sail across the Pacific in search of the southern landmass which previous explorers had found. Cook wanted to find out whether the places discovered were all part of one large continent or separate islands.

On October 7, 1769, they sighted New Zealand. In the next six months, they sailed around it, exploring the coastline and coming into contact with the native people, the Maoris, who lived there. The map Cook drew of the coastline proved that New Zealand was made up of two separate islands. The channel between the North and the South Islands is now called Cook Strait.

Australia sighted

On March 31, 1770, the *Endeavour* sailed west from New Zealand across the Tasman Sea, and on April 9, a

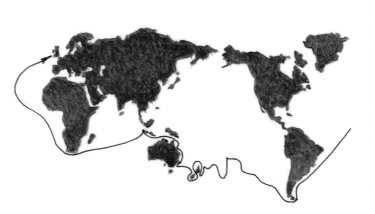

Cook's route around the world
1768–71. On his first expedition, which was to carry out scientific work in the South Seas and to search for a vast southern continent, he passed round Cape Horn at the southern tip of South America. He reached New Zealand in 1769 and Australia in 1770.

In all, Cook made three voyages to the Pacific. He found the maps of the Pacific not very accurate but, using scientific methods, was able to chart accurately the coastlines of a great number of islands.

He was the first European to visit a number of Pacific islands, including the Cook Islands, New Caledonia and the Hawaiian Islands (which he named the Sandwich Islands).

While looking for a northern sea passage between Europe and Asia, he became the first European to land on Vancouver Island on the northwest coast of North America.

sandy coast was sighted. It was the east coast of Australia.

Cook sailed north until he reached a large bay where they could anchor. They saw native people fishing in bark canoes, but the natives ignored the newcomers. A party went ashore and began to explore and, to their astonishment, they found a land rich in wildlife that was completely different from anything they had seen before. One of the team, Joseph Banks, collected thousands of plants, while another, Sydney Parkinson, drew the animals and plants they found. The wildlife was so rich that Cook named the place Botany Bay.

The *Endeavour* is holed
From Botany Bay, Cook sailed northwards, and by June he reached the Great Barrier Reef. But the *Endeavour* became stuck on a coral reef

and Cook ordered that heavy items should be thrown overboard to get the ship floating again. The plan worked, but the ship had a large hole in its side. He managed to beach the ship and repair it before setting sail again. He passed Cape York, the northern-most tip of Australia, where he landed and claimed the whole coastline for Britain.

By now the crew was tired and ill and the ship was badly battered. So Cook set sail for home and reached England in July 1771.

Cook made a second voyage of exploration between 1772 and 1775, when he explored the Antarctic Ocean and the Pacific islands, and again landed on New Zealand.

In July 1776, he set out for a third time with two ships – the *Resolution* and the *Discovery*. Once again he sailed to New Zealand and then set out on an

FASCINATING FACTS

The first European to discover Australia was a Dutchman, Willem Janszoon, who found Cape York in northern Australia in 1605. He named his discovery New Holland.

❑

In 1642, another Dutchman, Abel Tasman, sailed right round Australia without sighting land. He landed on the island now called Tasmania and explored the western coastline of New Zealand.

❑

Cook was determined that his men would not suffer from scurvy, a disease caused by a lack of vitamins, which had killed many sailors in the past. He made them drink lots of orange and lemon juice to provide vitamin C.

The Maoris had settled on the islands of New Zealand in about 1100. They were expert farmers, fishermen and canoe-builders. The first Maoris that Cook's party met were hostile, but the sailors later managed to trade with them. Many of the Maoris had colored tattoos on their bodies. Some of the sailors copied this idea.

❑

The Aborigines had come to Australia from southeastern Asia about 20,000 years before any Europeans arrived.

❑

Australia was used as a penal colony at first – a place where convicts were shipped from Britain. Many thousands were "transported" there.

Joseph Banks (1744–1820), the botanist.

unsuccessful search for the northwest passage around North America from the Pacific to the Atlantic oceans. On the way he became the first European to visit some of the Cook Islands and the Hawaiian Islands. In March 1778, he reached the North American coast and charted it as far north as the Bering Strait until he was forced back by icy seas. He then sailed south to spend the winter in Hawaii where he was killed in a dispute between his crew and the islanders.

Cook's place in history

Captain Cook did not discover Australia or New Zealand. He did not even sail right around Australia, so he did not know how big it was or gain an idea of its shape. But his achievements are a major turning point because he opened up a continent which no one knew anything about.

He identified the separate landmasses of New Zealand and Australia. The drawings and notes brought back by the scientists on the expedition told people about the environment of Australia with its extraordinary range of unique wildlife.

This Australian plant was named Banksia serata *after the botanist, Joseph Banks.*

Famine Among the Irish

A gaunt specter stalked the green hills of Ireland in the 1840s. Its name was Famine – and little was done to help its hapless victims. Nearly a million Irish people died and another million emigrated. They left for Britain, for America, for Australia, for anywhere so long as they could escape the meager crops and diseased potatoes, the grasping landlords and oppressive laws of Ireland.

800	400	BC/AD	400	800	1200	1600	2000

1842 Ireland

In the early nineteenth century, there was a period of crisis in Ireland. Until about 1740, the population of the country had been thinly scattered. Then the number of people living there began to rise. The Irish farmers now had to grow more food – mainly grain and the staple crop, potatoes. They produced more than enough to feed the Irish people and began to sell the surplus food to the British. At this time, many of the Irish people began to enjoy a better standard of living.

A change

The situation began to change in the nineteenth century when Britain started to buy grain from other European countries rather than Ireland. There was still a large Irish population to feed, but the land had been farmed so intensively that the soil was exhausted and the farmers could

not grow the good crops of the previous years.

The landowners then tried to take back much of their land by forcing their tenants – farmers who paid a rent for the land they farmed – to exist on tiny plots of land where they could hardly grow enough to feed their families.

Disaster!

The situation got worse as the population continued to grow. And then the crops began to fail. In 1845, there was a very poor potato crop. In 1846, it failed altogether. Because the farmers had no stores of food to fall back on, life became desperate.

There was a reasonable potato crop in 1847, but then it failed again in the following year. The people were starving and diseases,

Death claimed almost a million victims when the potato crop, on which many people in Ireland relied, failed and caused widespread starvation.

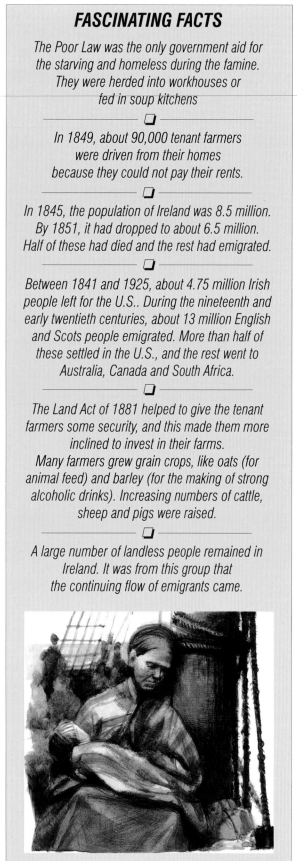

Irish emigrants on a ship to North America.

such as typhus, scurvy and dysentery, began to take a firm hold. The tenant farmers had to pay rents to their landlords. This was hard enough at the best of times, but now it was impossible.

Many could not pay and lost their land. By 1851, about two million people had disappeared from their farms. About half of these had died from starvation and disease, and the rest moved to Britain, North America and Australia. The large Irish communities in North America and Australia date from this wave of emigration during the years of famine.

Changes in Ireland

The famine years changed Ireland completely. In the past, there had always been two very different classes of people – the rich landowners and the poor tenant farmers. Now a new class of tenant farmers began to emerge. Many were better educated than the tenant farmers of old and they now had larger farms to work. They were able to make a profit from their produce and so their aims were similar to the landowners.

These farmers were not just trying to survive, and they began to farm with profit in mind. Some of their land was turned over to grass for animals, and the farmers began to export meat. They became more prosperous again.

Most people in Ireland were farmers surviving on tiny plots of land. They had no food supplies to fall back on when the potato crop failed, and the result was hunger and death for millions of people. To escape the dreadful conditions, many of those that survived left Ireland to live in another country. To most it did not matter where they went – they had little to lose.

Marx's Communist Manifesto

10-hour work days – low wages – dangerous machines – sacked if you fell ill: those were common working conditions in the mid-nineteenth century. Revolution was in the air; workers were joining together in trade unions to fight for better terms. Marx wrote his Manifesto against this background. Ignored at the time, it inspired many future leaders.

800	400	BC/AD	400	800	1200	1600	2000

1848 London, England

During the Industrial Revolution, which began in Britain in about 1750 and spread to other European countries in the nineteenth century, many people turned to industry rather than farming to make a living

As more factories sprang up, two new classes of people emerged. One was the huge army of working-class men and women who were needed to work the machines in the factories. The other was made up of the middle-class men who owned the factories.

Worker unrest
The factory bosses became rich, but they paid the workers low wages for working long hours in difficult conditions. The workers resented this, and many were ready to fight the factory owners for better pay and conditions. This was the

Karl Marx (1818–83) and Friedrich Engels (1820–95) (top). Engels managed a factory in Manchester and introduced Marx to the working-class movement in Britain.

background of unrest against which Karl Marx and Friedrich Engels wrote the *Communist Manifesto* in 1848.

Marx was a German philosopher and revolutionary. He left Germany in 1842 and lived in Paris, where he met Engels, another German. Marx later moved to Brussels, and then to London where he lived for the rest of his life. Engels also came to live in England and worked with Marx on many of his writings.

In the *Communist Manifesto* Marx and Engels traced the development of the capitalist bosses – those who supported the system in which the country's wealth is owned by individuals,

The spread of the Industrial Revolution led to the exploitation of most working people who were badly paid and lived in slum houses.

and not the state. They also showed how the power of the capitalists increased as they became richer. They predicted that the workers would organize themselves into trade unions to fight for better wages, and that some of the capitalists would join the workers in their fight. Then there would be a revolution, which would replace the capitalist system with communism.

The *Communist Manifesto* did not make much of an impression when it was written. A wave of revolutions swept through Europe in the early nineteenth century, but they were not inspired by communist ideals. The first communist revolution happened in Russia in 1917, which then became the Soviet

Union. Other eastern and central European countries also adopted a communist system of government.

In the second half of the nineteenth century, several socialist parties emerged in Europe. Socialists preferred reform to revolution, but they too wanted an end to individual ownership of wealth.

The basis of communist and socialist ideals – that a political party must work for the good of the people as a whole – has its roots in the theories put forward in the *Communist Manifesto*.

Most workers in the nineteenth century could be sacked on an employer's whim. A sacked worker often had great difficulty in finding another job.

Dunant & the Red Cross

Blood soaked the ground, moans filled the air – on every side lay the dead and dying. This was beyond enduring for one Swiss businessman caught up in the Battle of Solferino. He helped the wounded as best he could and came away determined that these horrors should never happen again. Four years later in Geneva, the International Red Cross was born.

800	400	BC/AD	400	800	1200	1600	2000

1863 Geneva, Switzerland

The International Red Cross & Red Crescent Movement, which helps millions of people across the world, was set up as the result of one man's reaction to the lack of medical help after a battle.

In 1859, a bitter war was raging in northern Italy. The Italian state of Sardinia-Piedmont had allied itself with France against their mutual enemy, Austria. They fought terrible battles at Magenta and Solferino in northern Italy. About 300,000 men fought at the Battle of Solferino. Of these, 40,000 were seriously injured or died. When the battle ended, there were hardly any medical supplies, very little food and no water.

Shocking scenes

A Swiss businessman, Henri Dunant, was caught up in this battle. He had arrived in Solferino the day before

Henri Dunant (1828–1910) was so shocked by the lack of medical help for wounded soldiers after a battle that he founded an agency devoted to helping humanity.

the battle. Dunant was shocked at the lack of medical care and tried to organize some help for the dying and wounded. But he felt that he must tell the world about the horrors he had witnessed.

So he wrote a book, *A Memory of Solferino*, in which he suggested that every country should have a group of volunteers who would provide medical aid for the armed forces in wartime.

Invitation to speak

One of the first people to read Dunant's book was a lawyer from Geneva, Gustave Moynier. He had experience performing charitable work and the ability to set up a team with the skills required for Dunant's proposal.

He asked Dunant to come to a meeting of the Geneva Public Welfare Society, of which he was chairman, and put forward his ideas.

This meeting in February 1863 led to the setting up of the five-man committee that was to form the Red Cross. Dunant and Moynier chose people with medical or military experience to serve on the committee.

International conferences

The five-man committee planned an international conference, to be held in Geneva, Switzerland, in October 1863. Representatives from sixteen nations attended the conference and, as a result, the first national societies came into being. The meeting also recommended that a diplomatic conference should be held to discuss Dunant's idea that the wounded on the battlefield should be given neutral status and that those who go to their aid should not be attacked.

This diplomatic conference was held in Geneva in 1864, and on August 22, 1864 the first Geneva Convention was signed by twelve governments. The convention outlined the way in which the relief organization should work. It has operated ever since.

Wounded to be protected

Representatives of the governments present at the convention pledged that sick and wounded soldiers, whatever their nationality, should be respected and cared for; that the people looking after them, the buildings sheltering them, the equipment needed to help them, and the transport used to move them should be protected. It was also agreed that a red cross on a white background should be the symbol of the new organization.

The committee in Geneva became known as the International Committee

FASCINATING FACTS

In time of war, the symbol of the red cross is used to protect doctors and nurses from attack by showing that they are not taking sides. The red cross represents the Swiss flag with its colors reversed.

❑

Muslim countries use the symbol of a crescent, and their relief organizations are known as Red Crescent Societies.

❑

Henri Dunant was awarded the first Nobel Peace Prize in 1901 for his work on founding the Red Cross.

Clara Barton (1821–1912) was an American school teacher who visited Europe and worked for the Red Cross in the Franco-Prussian War (1870–71). Back in the U.S., she founded the American Red Cross Society in 1881.

The Geneva Conventions were expanded to include caring for naval casualties (1907), prisoners of war (1929) and civilians in wartime (1949).

❑

The International Red Cross & Red Crescent Movement is staffed mainly by volunteers. It won the Nobel Peace Prize in 1917 and 1944. Worldwide, national membership is now over 250 million people.

❑

Representatives from twelve nations signed the first Geneva Convention in 1864. Today, 165 nations have signed it.

There are national Red Cross societies in almost every country in the world. Muslim countries use the name and emblem of a Red Crescent. Russia uses the Red Cross and Red Crescent together. In Iran they use a Red Lion & Sun.

of the Red Cross. It has twenty-five members, all of whom are Swiss. As Switzerland is a neutral country, it never takes part in wars, so its citizens can work with both sides in a conflict.

From Afghanistan to Zimbabwe

The number of national Red Cross societies increased steadily in the years following the first convention – the British Red Cross society was formed in 1870, the U.S. society in 1881, and the Australian Red Cross at the start of the First World War in 1914.

The work of the Red Cross has expanded into helping people in peacetime as well as war. This includes helping the victims of disasters like famines, floods, earthquakes and hurricanes. The Red Cross also looks after the sick, elderly and disabled, and runs blood banks, ambulances and health programs.

Societies in developing countries with poor resources, limited means and few technical staff receive help in the form of training officers, nurses, volunteers, advice and materials. The size and scope of its work has grown far beyond the wildest dreams of the man who witnessed the terrible scenes of bloodshed at the Battle of Solferino.

The Red Cross & Red Crescent work for the relief of human suffering all over the world, in peace as well as war. Members are pledged to help those in need, regardless of their race, religion, color or sexual orientation.

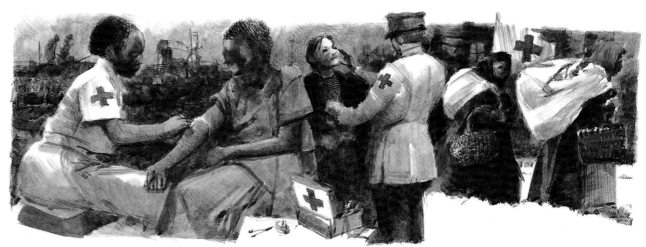

Freud Interprets Dreams

"People have thoughts they don't know they are thinking!" said Freud in 1899. His study of how the human mind works showed him that what went on in people's heads was far more complicated than had been imagined up to then. His work changed how we think of ourselves and made us far more aware of how we might help the mentally ill.

800	400	BC/AD	400	800	1200	1600		2000

1895 Vienna, Austria

In the early twentieth century, a group of doctors made some startling discoveries which changed the way people thought about the mind and how it worked. Perhaps the best known of these men is Sigmund Freud, but others, such as Carl Jung and Alfred Adler, also made significant contributions to the science that came to be known as psychoanalysis. This is a method of finding out about the unconscious part of a person's mind and using this knowledge to treat mental disorders.

Revealing the unconscious
Conscious thoughts are the ones which you know about. Unconscious thoughts are the ones which you do not know about – they are going on deep in your mind. Some of the methods psychoanalysts use to bring these unconscious thoughts to the surface

Sigmund Freud (1856–1939) was one of the pioneers of psychoanalysis. Some of his views were controversial and led to disagreements with fellow analysts.

include questioning, free association and hypnosis. In free association, the patient speaks all of his or her thoughts aloud. This gives the psychoanalyst clues about what is going on in the unconscious part of the patient's mind.

Sigmund Freud, an Austrian, studied medicine and then, in 1882, he joined the staff of a psychiatric clinic – a hospital for mentally ill patients – in Vienna, Austria. His work with these patients brought him to the conclusion that many mental disorders were due to childhood experiences, either real or imagined.

The meaning of dreams
In 1899, he wrote a book, *The Interpretation of Dreams*, in which he analyzed dreams to show how they related to desires and experiences – events in which people are involved – that are unconscious and often

dating from childhood. This whole idea of the unconscious part of the mind and the effect it has on our conscious thoughts and behavior was a completely new idea.

Other people began to follow Freud's ideas and gather at his house to discuss psychoanalysis. Two of these people were Carl Jung and Alfred Adler. Jung was a Swiss psychiatrist who introduced the idea of "introvert" and "extrovert" personalities. People with introvert personalities withdraw into themselves and do not seem to take much interest in the outside world.

Extroverts are interested in the outside world and are outgoing and talkative. Classifying personalities in

Carl Jung (1875–1961) made an important contribution to psychoanalysis.

this way helps people to understand each other's behavior.

Adler (1870–1937), another Austrian, came up with the theory of the "inferiority complex" to explain certain types of behavior. An inferiority complex is a belief that someone is less worthwhile than other people in some way. This can lead to aggressive behavior.

Many of Freud's original theories were later altered, but they did shed light on the workings of the mind. Until then, people did not realize that there was an unconscious part which affected human behavior. The ideas of Freud and other important psychoanalysts have changed our understanding of ourselves and influenced thinking in all walks of life.

Europe Colonizes Africa

Africa was the unknown continent to most Europeans in the nineteenth century. Then, from about 1880, European countries began building empires in these untouched lands. They wanted the minerals, wood and other natural resources to feed their industries. European inventions and medicines hardly made up for the way that Africans and their lands were exploited and their way of life destroyed.

800	400	BC/AD	400	800	1200	1600	2000

1908 Kinshasa, Zaire

Even by the second half of the nineteenth century, very little was known about Africa. Some gold had been exported from West Africa by Portuguese traders in the fifteenth and sixteenth centuries. And when Europeans set up cotton and sugar plantations in the New World from the sixteenth century, millions of slaves were sent from the coastal regions of Africa to North America to work for them. But, for the Europeans, much of the rest of Africa was a mystery.

The race to explore Africa
And then suddenly, in the 1870s, the countries of Europe began a race to explore Africa. By the end of the century, they had conquered most of the continent, set up thirty new colonies and changed the way of life of 110 million African

Leopold of the Belgians (1835–1909) wanted to increase his country's importance by establishing a new colony in Africa. He sponsored Stanley's exploration of the Congo.

people. So what started this rush?

In the nineteenth century, several British explorers had ventured into Africa. The most famous of these was David Livingstone (1813–73) who spent thirty years in Africa and died there. During that time, he was the first European to discover a great river, the Lualaba, in Central Africa, as well as exploring stretches of the Zambezi, Shire and Rovuma rivers, Lake Ngami, the Victoria Falls and Lake Nyasa (now Malawi).

Leopold's dream
However, one man, Leopold II, King of Belgium, stands out as being the leader in the race – he had a dream of setting up a colony for Belgium in Africa. In 1876, he read of a British explorer, Verney Cameron, who claimed that the Lualaba turned

The Europeans came upon civilizations which they knew nothing about or refused to believe were African. They did not believe that the stone ruins known as Great Zimbabwe were built by local people. Some believed they were the mythical site of King Solomon's mines. Others thought that Arabs from northern Africa had built them.

Europeans did not think of the Egyptians as Africans, but as a separate civilization who were more like Europeans. But the Egyptians were Africans who had strong connections with Nubia to the south, and they occupied the region from about 2000 BC. Nubian kings later dominated Egypt.

About ten million African slaves were exported to America before the slave trade was banned in 1807. But it was not until 1865, the end of the American Civil War, that slavery became illegal throughout America.

David Livingstone discovered that quinine could combat malaria. Before this, malaria had killed many explorers in tropical Africa.

The Egyptian sun-god, Horus.

to the west and became the river Congo. He described a land rich in minerals which just needed money to exploit it.

Leopold was a very rich man, but before he would commit himself to a venture he needed to find out if Cameron's account was accurate. He invited several well-known explorers and representatives from European nations to a conference on opening up Africa and bringing Christianity to its people. As a result, many Europeans saw Leopold as the leader of an international crusade.

But Britain felt she had a right to the

Part of the ruins at Great Zimbabwe.

continent because she had led the exploration of Africa and the spread of Christianity. Other countries, particularly France, disagreed. The rush to colonize Africa was on.

Leopold knew that the Welsh explorer, Henry Stanley (1841–1904), had set out in 1875 to follow the Lualaba all the way to the sea and prove that it was the Congo. Inspired by his explorations, Leopold employed Stanley in 1879 to open up the land drained by the Congo for the Belgians.

After fighting off rival European claims, Leopold established the Congo Free State and, in

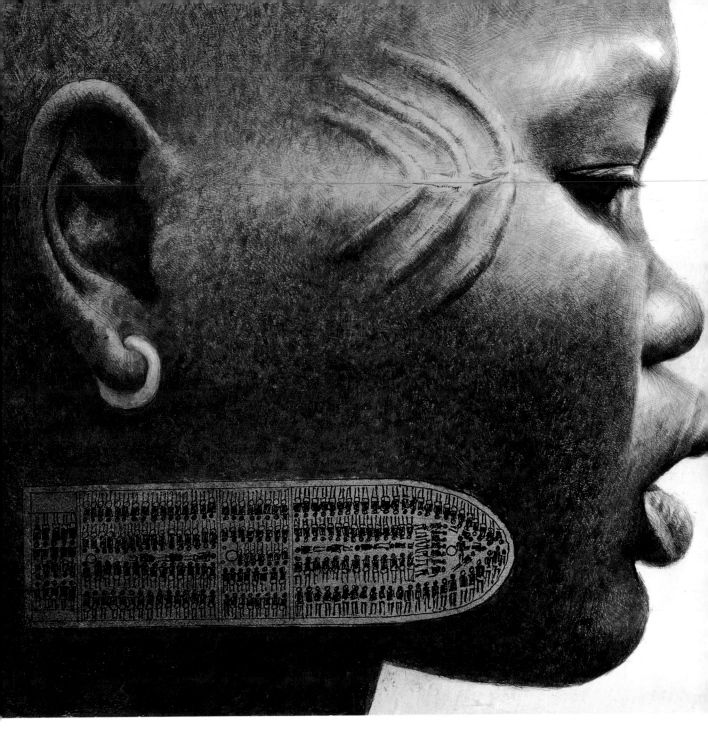

1908, the colony was named the Belgian Congo. By 1914, the whole of Africa was divided into colonies and protectorates (countries which are partly governed and defended by another country), except for Ethiopia, Liberia, and the Union of South Africa.

Fight for freedom
However, after World War II (1939–45), there was a move by African countries to become independent or free of European control. In 1958, the first Conference of Independent African States was held in Ghana with eight states attending. By 1960, there were 27 independent countries in Africa. The number of countries gaining independence was now rising rapidly, and by 1977, the last territory under direct European rule became independent.

However, in 1993, South Africa was still ruled by its European minority,

although the "apartheid" system of racial segregation had mostly been dismantled. The proposed new constitution and government would at last give the black majority a say in running their country.

By imposing their religions and culture on the native Africans, the Europeans destroyed much of the African traditional way of life that had existed for thousands of years. Yet they brought many benefits, such as

In the late 19th century, Africa was quickly developed into a vast empire of colonies under European rule. The British and South African statesman, Cecil Rhodes (1853–1902), tried to build an empire for Great Britain "from Cape to Cairo." He also endowed the Rhodes Scholarships for American students to Oxford.

modern medicine, transport, and industry. Today, the African nations have their freedom, but the years of colonization have left a deep mark.

The Wall Street Crash

"Stock Market Crashes!" – "Prominent Banker Suicides!" – "Millions Ruined!"
The screaming newspaper headlines said it all in October 1929.
Across the world, companies went bankrupt and workers lost their jobs.
Every country in the world was affected, every industry, every household – the
misery caused inspired Roosevelt's "New Deal" and the British Welfare State.

800	400	BC/AD	400	800	1200	1600	2000

1929 New York, USA

After the First World War, the U.S. seemed to be on the road to economic success. Industry boomed as factories made such items as cars and stoves. The majority of people could find work, and people who invested in shares in the new industries were making fortunes.

But then, in 1929, everything suddenly crashed. This was the start of the Depression – a worldwide slump in trade when businesses collapsed and millions of people were out of work. Why did this happen?

Danger signs
The situation in the U.S. was not as rosy as it seemed on the surface. There was plenty of work around, but the wages of most people were not keeping pace with the price of goods.

Franklin D. Roosevelt (1882–1945), president of the U.S. (1933–45), was paralyzed from the waist down by polio, but was still the only U.S. president to be re-elected three times.

So Americans could not afford to buy enough goods to expand the home market.

Meanwhile, Europe was recovering after the war. American goods were exported to Europe, and European countries also relied on loans of money from the U.S. to boost their industries and buy the goods they needed. If the U.S. needed its money back at any time, world trade would collapse.

Between 1925 and 1928, the price of shares

People lining up at a soup kitchen. During the "Crash," investment in industry fell sharply, and many people had less money to spend because they had lost their savings. More and more people were forced out of work and had to rely on handouts in order to survive. Roosevelt's policies helped the U.S. to recover from the Depression.

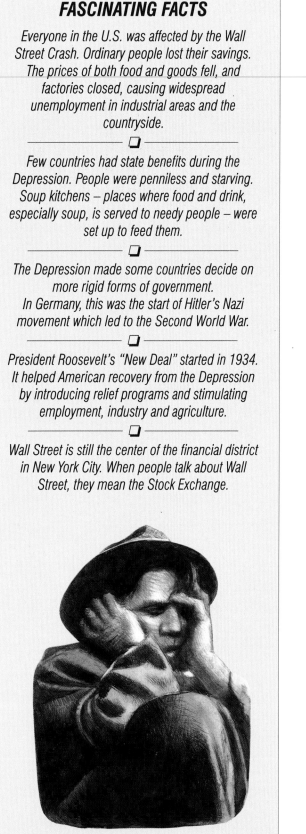

Thousands of U.S. farmers lost their land.

continued to rise as business boomed. At the Stock Exchange on Wall Street, people were rushing to buy shares, hoping to sell them for a large profit. This pushed share prices up and up. People used their life savings or borrowed money to buy shares thinking they would be able to pay it back when they made their fortunes.

The Crash

The tide turned in October 1929. People had become nervous that the upward trend would not continue and were selling their shares. Now there were more people selling than buying, and share prices began to fall.

Events were happening so fast that it was difficult to tell how much price levels were falling. Thou.s.nds of people decided to sell while they still had some money – or so they thought. But prices had fallen far more sharply than people realized. Panic set in as share prices tumbled. On October 24, 1929, nearly thirteen million people sold their shares for much lower prices than they thought possible. Many people faced ruin.

The world suffers

Countries which had borrowed money from the U.S. were badly affected, too. They had to pay back their loans to the U.S., and all over the world investors lost their money, businesses crashed and millions lost their jobs. Overseas trade almost ceased and industrial production dropped.

The Depression affected all countries and eventually changed world trade because countries had to rely on themselves to produce goods – they could no longer depend on help from elsewhere.

King Marches for Civil Rights

"Just like the rock that stands by the water's side, we shall not be moved," sang the marchers in the U.S. in the 1960s. They were determined to abolish the discrimination against African Americans, known as segregation, which made Black people into second-class citizens. Led by the inspirational preacher, Martin Luther King Jr., they shamed Americans into changing the unjust laws.

| 800 | 400 | BC/AD | 400 | 800 | 1200 | 1600 | 2000 |

1965 Atlanta, Georgia, USA

The Black Africans who were shipped to the U.S. from the sixteenth century onwards, were sold to White European settlers as slaves. The slaves were often treated with great cruelty – they had no rights and the slave owners had the power of life and death over them.

After slavery was abolished in the U.S. in 1865, Black people were supposed to be free, but they had no land and no power. They were treated as second-class citizens, who were separated from White people and they had to work for very low wages.

Equal rights

Black people had no hope of change unless there was a proper movement to win them equal rights with Whites. Many people fought for the rights of Black people, but the contribution of one man stands out from the others. His name was

Martin Luther King Jr. (1929–68) was an outstanding speaker, who believed in nonviolent protest. He organized peaceful demonstrations against racial inequality.

Martin Luther King Jr. King was born in Atlanta, Georgia, in 1929. His father was a minister in the Baptist church. From him, King learned that the church bound the Black community together and that a church leader could have great influence.

King becomes a minister

King decided to become a minister like his father and began to preach at his father's church. He left to study at Boston University in the northeastern state of Massachusetts, where he was awarded a doctorate in theology. He then became a minister in the town of Montgomery, in the southern state of Alabama. It was here that he was to lead a major battle for civil rights.

Conditions were particularly bad for Black people in the South. Black and White

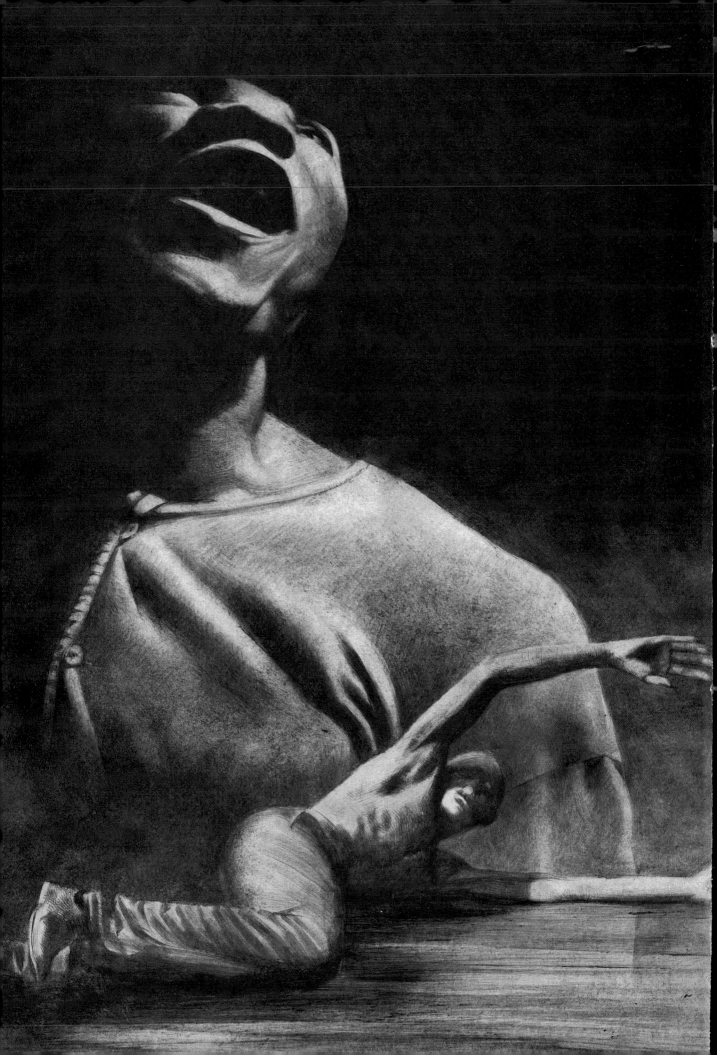

children had to attend different schools. They even had to sit in different parts of the bus. One day in 1955, a Black woman in the town of Montgomery refused to give up her seat for a White person, and she was arrested. After this, all the Black people in the town refused to use the buses in protest.

About 17,500 Black people normally used the buses, which was three-quarters of all passengers. The boycott lasted for months, until segregation on the buses ended. This success was only a start, but it gave hope to thou.s.nds of Black people in other towns in the South.

Vicious attacks

King was asked to speak at meetings all over the U.S.. However, many White people in the South wanted segregation to continue.

Birmingham, Alabama was one of the most violently racist cities, where White people put up fierce resistance to any reforms. King and his team decided to take on Birmingham. They staged sit-ins and

Some Black leaders believed that they should meet violence from Whites – many Black people were hanged and burned alive by the Ku Klux Klan, for example – with violence. But King believed that peaceful demonstrations and speeches were the way to bring segregation and injustice to the notice of the world.

The Ku Klux Klan was a secret organization of Whites who committed terrible crimes in their fight against equal rights for Blacks.

boycotts in an effort to persuade the city to stop segregation and give Black people better jobs.

The authorities fought back and King was arrested. However, he was soon released and gathered massive support from the Black community to join in the demonstrations. The police turned high-pressure hoses on the demonstrators. The powerful jets of water knocked people over and tore their clothes. Some of the demonstrators tried to fight back, but the police released fierce dogs into the crowd to terrify the marchers.

Meanwhile, the, whole scene was being recorded by television cameras. The next day, people all over the U.S. saw these vicious attacks and they were shocked. White people all over the country began to support the Black's call for reforms, and President Kennedy intervened to force the local people to accept some of the demonstrators' demands.

King's dream

In August 1963, 200,000 people marched in Washington to support a bill – an early version of a law before it is passed by Congress and becomes an Act – for civil rights. King decided to turn the occasion into a national movement for Black civil rights. And there, at the Lincoln Memorial, King made his greatest speech of all:

"I have a dream that one day this nation will rise up and live out the true meaning of its creed: 'We hold these truths to be self-evident, that all men are created equal.'….

I have a dream that one day on the red hills of Georgia, sons of former slaves and sons of former slave-owners will be able to sit down together at the table of brotherhood….

I have a dream that one day even the state of Mississippi will be transformed into an oasis of freedom and justice…."

The crowd roared as he finished his speech and King was later pronounced the unofficial "President of Black America." There was still more work to do but on July 2, 1964, President Johnson signed the Civil Rights Act.

King went on to lead a drive for Black voting rights and then turned his attention to poverty among blacks and racial discrimination in housing. He was murdered in Memphis, Tennessee, in 1968 soon after making another great speech.

More than 100,000 people attended his funeral in Atlanta. M.L. King's achievements did not end racism in the U.S., but the movement had helped civil rights worldwide.

King made his electrifying "I have a dream" speech at the Lincoln Memorial in Washington. He spoke of his dream of an America free from racial discrimination.

Further Reading

Brown, Julie, and Robert Brown. *Explorers*. London: Belitha Press, 1990.

Brown, Pam. *Henry Dunant*. Watford, England: Exley, 1988.

Clarke, Fiona. *Greece in the Time of Pericles*. New York: Simon and Schuster, 1993.

Davidso, Basil. *Africa in History*. New York: Collier, 1991.

Davis, W. S. *A Day in Old Athens*. Cheshire, CT: Biblo & Tannen, N.d.

Dawson, Raymond. *Confucius*. New York: Oxford University Press, 1981.

Dodge, Stephen C. *Christopher Columbus and the First Voyages to the New World*. New York: Chelsea House, 1991.

Fuson, Robert H., trans. *The Log of Christopher Columbus*. Camden, ME: International Marine, 1987.

Hamey, David. *Captain James Cook and the Explorers of the Pacific*. New York: Chelsea House, 1991.

Harris, Nathaniel. *The Great Depression*. North Pomfret, VT: David & Charles, 1988.

Israel, Fred L. *Franklin Delano Roosevelt*. New York: Chelsea House, 1985.

Jakoubek, Robert E. *Martin Luther King*. New York: Chelsea House, 1989.

Martell, Hazel Mary. *The Ancient Chinese*. Portsmouth, NH: Heinemann, 1992.

Millard, Anne. *The Usborne Book of World History*. Tulsa, OK: Usborne, 1985.

Morris, Scott, ed. *Religions of the World*. New York: Chelsea House, 1993.

Naipaul, V. S. *Among the Believers: An Islamic Journey*. New York: Knopf, 1981.

Pierre, Michel. *The Renaissance*. Edited by Walter Kossmann. Lexington, MA: Silver, 1987.

Powers, Elizabeth. *Nero*. New York: Chelsea House, 1988.

Ross, Nancy Wilson. *Buddhism: A Way of Life and Thought*. New York: Knopf, 1981.

Santi, Bruno. *Leonardo da Vinci*. New York: SCALA/Riverside, 1990.

Schulke, Flip, and Penelope McPhee. *King Remembered*. New York: Pocket, 1986.

Scott, John Anthony. *Settlers on the Eastern Shore*. New York: Facts on File, 1991.

Smart, Ninian. *The Long Search*. Boston: Little, Brown, 1977.

Stefoff, Rebecca. *Marco Polo and the Medieval Explorers*. New York: Chelsea House, 1992.

Stepanek, Sally. *Martin Luther*. New York: Chelsea House, 1986.

Storr, Anthony. *Freud*. New York: Oxford University Press, 1989.

Ventura, Piero. *Michelangelo's World*. New York: Putnam, 1988.

Index